1,000 Ra[...]
Everyone S[...]ld [...]ow

A collection of random facts useful for the bar trivia night, get-together or as conversation starter.

2

1,000 Random Facts Everyone Should Know

Have you ever had that moment when you are in the middle of a conversation and suddenly the room becomes quiet and nobody knows how to move the discussion forward? Have you ever wondered why people can effortlessly drive conversations by dropping quirky and weird tidbits here and there to keep people interested and engaged?

Have you ever had moments when you wish you knew something that others don't, so you can catch their attention and command the room? Of course, you do. Haven't we all? It's for this reason that we decided to write this book.

You never know when some of these facts can come in handy as a conversation starter or something that you can use to move the conversation along. You never know when you can use these facts to pick up girls, or for girls to one-up men who think they know everything. Besides, it's just plain fun reading about these quirky and weird facts that range from funny to downright surprising.

Whatever your motivation is, there's a really good chance that you'll find these facts and tidbits useful; or, it's also possible that you'll find these facts useless, but then again, isn't that what the internet is for?

So if you're ready, here are 1,000 facts that everyone should know about, dig in!

Animals

1. Feathered trafficking? Macaws are popular pets, but many species of macaw are endangered in the wild. This endangered status has led to laws forbidding wild capture and importation, making illegal trafficking of these birds on the black market a lucrative business.

2. Here's a fact to bring to your next Thanksgiving dinner: Though the 'gobble gobble' sound is associated with all turkeys, typically it is only the male making this sound. Male turkeys perfect their unique 'gobble' sounds for turkey mating habits.

3. Contrary to Dracula's claims, vampire bats DO want to suck your blood, but are far more likely to feed on cattle and horses than people. The bite of a vampire bat will not drain its victim of enough blood to cause harm, but can cause a nasty infection.

4. Cockatiels are monogamous birds that pair off young and remain loyal to each other throughout the year. Though already paired up, they still engage in vocalizations and body language of mating rituals when mating season begins.

5. Domestic cats spend over 50% of their lives asleep, but some large cats sleep even more than that. Lions and tigers can sleep up to 20 hours a day.

6. Trying to sneak up on a turkey? Good luck! They have periscopic vision because of the placement of their eyes on the side of their head. This gives turkeys a 360-degree range of vision.

7. Heroes come in all sizes... and species! Scarlett, a Brooklyn cat living with her litter in an abandoned building, had to move quickly when fire threatened the lives of her kittens. The New York Daily News reported that she fought through the fire and suffered from severe burns, but Scarlett still managed to carry out each of her five kittens out of the burning building. She and all but one of her kittens survived due to her quick reaction and tenacity.

8. Even though they're native to the Andes Mountains, almost all chinchillas sold in the United States are direct descendants of the original eleven that Mathias Chapman, an American mining engineer, brought from South America in the early 20s.

9. A cow has to pump 400 pints of blood through its udder to produce just one pint of milk. That's a 400:1 ratio!

10. In just one day, a cow can produce around 60 pounds of manure. If you do the math, that adds up to be over 20,000 pounds of manure every year from just one animal!

11. Putting nose rings in bulls is a method to help maintain control over the animal, which is the origin for the expression "to lead someone by the nose."

12. Cows in the cold are good for more than just their milk. It is reported that early forms of hockey were played with frozen cow dung for a puck!

13. Dogs love just like we do... chemically, at least. A recent study found that when dogs play with other animals, their brains release the same "love" hormone that humans release during intimate actions.

14. The Guinness World Record for "Smallest Working Dog" was awarded to a 2.5 pound Yorkie named Lucy. She lives in New Jersey and works as a therapy dog.

15. According to trainers, a reward for a dog's good behavior must occur within seconds. Otherwise, a dog may not correlate its good behavior with positive reinforcement.

16. North American porcupines may have upwards of 30,000 quills on their bodies.

17. Dogs are good for more than just companionship. Various published studies report that dogs have the ability to detect cancer, diabetes, and even epilepsy in humans. Dogs can be trained to sniff out different cancers including, skin, bladder, breast, and prostate cancer. They can smell when a diabetic person's blood sugar is too high or too low and can even predict an epileptic seizure 45 minutes prior to a human having a seizure.

18. Contrary to the popular belief, dogs do not see in black and white. They are able to see colors but have trouble distinguishing between certain colors. Their sight is better in lower light and detecting motion. These are qualities that may be of tremendous help when hunting.

19. The pharaohs of Ancient Egypt were often buried with their favorite dog, so that the dog could protect them in the afterlife.

20. The results of Bloodhound tracking are acceptable as evidence in nearly any court of law.

21. It is estimated that the nose of a bloodhound houses roughly 230 million scent receptors. This is 40 times the amount in the human nose. They also possess a relentless tracking drive and have been known to pursue a scent for over 130 miles, only stopping when it reaches the source of the scent or completely loses the trail.

22. Boxers are capable of holding down jobs that require extensive training. Boxers have been used as wartime couriers, seeing-eye dogs, and police dogs.

23. Dogs resembling Great Danes can be found in Egyptian art dating as far back as 3000 B.C.E.

24. The tallest recorded dog on record is a Great Dane named Zeus who is 44 inches from shoulders to ground, putting him at about the size of an average donkey.

25. Near the end of WWII, Germans began hiding their treasures across the borders to preserve them from their imminent defeat; this included not just art and gold, but many of their German Shorthaired Pointers!

26. The greyhound is the fastest breed of domestic dog, with maximum speeds of about 45 miles per hour.

27. Labrador Retrievers were used in their native Newfoundland as working dogs. Fishermen would use Labrador Retrievers to help capture fish from lines and to help pull in nets.

28. A monument to one pit bull hero was erected at Gettysburg. Sallie, a Staffordshire bull terrier, was present at the Battle of Gettysburg, standing guard over wounded Union soldiers.

29. A study by American Temperament Testing Society found the scores regarding the temperament of Staffordshire Bull Terriers and American Pit Bull Terriers, dogs that are commonly called "pit bulls", were shown to be more stable than the temperament of Golden Retrievers. Statistically, the most aggressive dog breeds tend to be small to medium-sized breeds such as Dachshunds, Chihuahuas, and Jack Russell Terriers.

30. The average weight of an adult horse's heart is about 10 pounds, which makes it about the size of a large melon!

31. Weimaraners can't get enough of their owners! They have been known to develop attachment issues resulting in separation anxiety and may cause trouble when left alone. They like to be so close to their owners that they've earned the nickname "Velcro dogs"!

32. One of the most famous Yorkies was a dog named Smoky who was a service dog during WWII. She helped string communication lines between outposts in the Philippines and worked as one of the first therapy dogs.

33. A dog's sense of smell puts ours to shame! Dogs have been estimated to smell somewhere between 10,000 to 100,000 times better than a human.

34. While efforts have been made, Zebras have never been fully domesticated. They have traits that are not exactly "people friendly". They can be savage biters and are able to kick with enough force to break a lion's jaw.

35. Zebra foals are able to walk within 20 minutes after being born and can run after an hour.

36. Goats have unique eyes. Their pupils are actually rectangular instead of round.

37. All of today's Percheron horses are related. Every one of them can trace their bloodline back to a single sire in the 19th century named Jean Le Blanc.

38. Adult horses can drink upwards of 12 gallons of water a day.

39. The Quarter Horse breed originally received its name because of its noted speed at one-quarter of a mile.

40. "You are NOT the father!" Socks, the moonwalking Shetland pony from the UK mobile phone advertisement, was caught in a paternity battle in June of 2013. After being put out to stud with three mares, he swam across a loch to mate with a mare on the other side. The mare subsequently gave birth and the paternity of her colt was tested, which revealed that Socks was not the father.

41. Horses have very powerful instincts. They can sense when their riders are feeling anxious or afraid, and often ignore or disobey their riders for this reason. Horses can even express jealousy and vengeance.

42. Even pigs can't resist bacon. Although they usually just nibble on each other's tails and ears, pigs have been known to cannibalize one another.

43. Pigs were domesticated about 10,000 years ago and today inhabit all continents except Antarctica.

44. Pigs may have a reputation for being dirty, but they're actually as clean as dogs and cats. Since they are unable to sweat, they roll in the mud too keep cool. This may have contributed to their filthy reputation.

45. A squealing pig can reach up to 115 decibels. That's louder than the Concorde Jet, which can reach up to 112 decibels.

46. Pigs have an uncanny sense of smell. They are able to detect scents 25 feet underground, which can be advantageous when searching for food.

47. During Woodrow Wilson's presidency, he and the First Lady kept grazing sheep on the front lawn of the White House in order to keep in neat and trimmed.

48. Some caribou herds migrate over 600 miles annually.

49. Bearded dragons perform one of the same gestures as us... they wave their arm! They will stand on three legs, lift the fourth, and wave it in a circular motion to acknowledge other dragons or diffuse aggression between them.

50. An adult sugar glider can weigh around 4 ounces and live up to 14 years. They can glide almost 150 feet.

51. The heart of a shrimp is located in its head.

52. Because they don't have thumbs like human babies, so baby elephants suck their trunks for comfort.

53. It is incredibly common for humans to be allergic to cats. But interestingly enough, some cats are allergic to humans!

54. Thousands of new trees are planted each year simply because squirrels forgot where they hid their acorns!

55. Who says "chivalry is dead?" When playing with female puppies, male puppies with often let them win. Even if they have a clear physical advantage.

56. There have been studies showing that goats have accents just like us!

57. As if we need another reason to fear sharks... Great white sharks can detect a drop of blood in 25 gallons of water and can even sense tiny amounts of blood from three miles away.

58. The Tesla Model S can go from zero to sixty miles per hour in just 2.28 seconds, narrowly beating a cheetah's ability to do it in three.

59. The colorfully beautiful, but deadly 2-inch-long golden poison dart frog has enough venom to kill 10 adult men.

60. African elephants have the longest pregnancy of any mammal... nearly two years long!

61. *Fugu*, or pufferfish meat, is a delicacy in Japan. If you want to try it, you better trust your chef! Almost all pufferfish contain a toxin called tetrodoxin, which is up to 1,200 times more lethal to humans than cyanide.

62. Wolves have a serious appetite! They can eat up to twenty pounds of meat in one sitting!

63. Just as no two snowflakes are identical, no two tigers have the same stripe pattern. Their stripes not only appear in their fur, but are imprinted onto their skin!

64. Alligators have been around for 150 million years, managing to avoid extinction 65 million years ago when their dinosaur pals died off.

65. Clearly, going to the dentist has never been fun. Ancient Greek dentists used the venom from stingrays as an anesthetic.

66. Giraffes and humans have the same number of bones in their neck.

67. Can you touch your tongue to your nose? A giraffe's tongue is so long that it uses it to clean its ears.

68. A newborn Chinese water deer is so small that it can be held in the palm of your hand.

69. Hummingbirds can fly backwards, upside down and even sideways! However, their tiny legs are too weak to support walking.

70. Here's a skill that all new parents wish they could obtain: Dolphins can stay active for 15 days or more by sleeping with only one half of their brain at a time.

71. Grizzly bear dads have been known to kill cubs, so protective moms find dens that are far away from males.

72. Ostriches can run faster than horses and male ostriches can roar like lions.

73. In Alaska, whispering in someone's ear while they are moose hunting can get you jail time!

74. Sharks have more reason to fear us than we do of them. Sharks kill fewer than 10 people per year. Humans kill about 100 million sharks per year.

75. Scientists have named chickens as the closest living relative to a Tyrannosaurus Rex.

76. Barn owls have a lower divorce rate than humans. They are normally monogamous, but about 25 percent of mated pairs split up.

77. A single strand of spider silk is thinner than a human hair, but five times stronger than steel of the same width. A spider silk rope just 2 inches thick could reportedly stop a Boeing 747.

78. Like the White Walkers in *Game of Thrones*, Reindeer eyeballs turn blue in winter to help them see at lower light levels. Enhanced night vision activates and a layer of tissue behind the retina makes them look blue. During the summer, their eyes reflect most of the light through the retina resulting in a golden appearance.

79. The Pacific Giant octopus has three hearts to accompany their eight tentacles! Two pump blood to the gills, while the third circulates blood to the rest of the body.

80. A blue whale's tongue is massive and can weigh as much as 8,000 pounds. That's as much as an elephant!

81. Diamonds aren't EVERY girl's best friend... Male penguins propose to females by giving them a pebble. Gentoo Penguins look for the smoothest, shiniest pebble to present to the female he chooses. If she accepts his proposal, she will place the pebble in her nest as a symbol of accepting him as her mate.

82. It's electric! The electric eel can deliver 600 volts of current. That's enough electricity to knock down a fully-grown horse!

83. Bad news for city dwellers: A cockroach can survive decapitation, but will die after a week out of hunger or thirst.

84. No dog left behind! African wild dogs are known for caring for the young, old and injured in their pack. They care for wounds by licking them and bring back food for the old and injured.

85. Rats are ticklish too! When tickled along their nape area, they emit ultrasonic sounds that can only heard by humans using special sound equipment.

86. Leeches have been used in medicine for over 2,500 years. They have three separate jaws, each with 100 tiny teeth to bite through skin and suck blood. Widely used in the 19th century, they are still utilized in parts of the world to heal wounds and restore circulation.

87. A starfish has five eyes. That's one for each leg. However, they can only detect light and darkness.

88. The fingerprints of a koala are so indistinguishable from humans that they have on occasion been confused at a crime scene.

89. Hippos secrete a reddish, oily fluid called "pink sweat" that contains a water-repellent, moisturizing sunblock that can also be utilized as an antibiotic!

90. Humans aren't the only ones known to fight over land. A super colony of invasive Argentine ants, known as the "California large", covers 560 miles of the U.S. West Coast. It's currently engaged in a turf war with a nearby super colony in Mexico.

91. Pandas can't get enough bamboo! It takes 28 pounds of bamboo to satisfy a giant panda's dietary needs.

92. The largest bald eagle nest on record was 20 feet high and weighed two tons.

93. It is unwise to pick a fight with a grizzly bear. Their bite is strong enough to crush a bowling ball!

94. The now extinct colossus penguin stood as tall as LeBron James!

95. Kangaroos use their tails for balance, so if you lift a kangaroo's tail off the ground, it can't hop.

96. Everyone needs a "bestie". Even cows have best friends!

97. A snail can sleep for three years.

98. Cats and horses are highly susceptible to black widow venom, but dogs are relatively resistant. Sheep and rabbits are apparently immune.

99. Elephants show tremendous empathy, even to other species. They mourn their dead and will put themselves in harm's way to help another animal.

100. In 1924, A Labrador Retriever was sentenced to life without parole at Eastern State Penitentiary for killing the Governor's cat.

History

101. In ancient Egypt, being a servant was not exactly the most appealing job. They were smeared with honey in order to attract flies away from the pharaoh. Their service didn't end after their pharaoh's death either. Some pharaoh's chose to be sealed in their tombs alongside their living servants, pets and concubines.

102. Albert Einstein was offered the role of Israel's second President in 1952, but declined.

103. Tea bags were accidentally invented in 1904. Thomas Sullivan found that it was cheaper to send samples to customers in bags instead of boxes. The customers thought they were meant to be dunked in hot water, which lead to requests for "tea bag" orders!

104. Fidel Castro once said, "If surviving assassination attempts were an Olympic event, I would win the gold medal". There were more than 600 plots to take his life.

105. The use of fingerprints to identify people began when two men who looked nearly identical, with the same name, arrived at the same prison. They had never even met!

106. Being buried alive was such a common occurrence in the 19th century that inventors created a "safety coffin". It allowed anyone waking up six-feet-under the ability to alert people above ground if they were still alive.

107. The Parliament of Iceland is the oldest legislature in the world. It was founded in 930.

108. The Civil War is often referred to as the bloodiest conflict in U.S. history. An 1889 study showed that approximately 620,000 soldiers died in the Civil War. Recent studies, however, put the number as high as 850,000.

109. Napoleon was once attacked by 1,000 rabbits.

110. Boston was in a very sticky situation in 1919 when a 90-foot wide tank exploded containing two and a half million gallons of molasses. The entire contents of the tank spilled in the streets at 35 miles per hour and up to 15 feet high. It demolished buildings, carried away vehicles, killed 21 people and injured 150. The cleanup took weeks.

111. Ronald Reagan was a lifeguard during high school and saved 77 lives. Though locals joke that many of those "survivors" were women faking distress to be rescued by the handsome lifeguard.

112. The phrase "pardon my French" used after swearing began in the 19th century. English-speaking people would use French phrases in conversation to display class, apologizing to the listeners unfamiliar with the language. They would hide swear words under the pretense of the words being a foreign language.

113. The Great Fire of London in 1666 caused terrible damage, destroying 13,200 homes in and St. Paul's Cathedral. Surprisingly, there were only six confirmed deaths.

114. There's a monster mushroom in Oregon that is 2,400 years old. It is still alive and growing today with a root system covering approximately three miles of land.

115. Noble life can get mundane. Marie Antoinette had a fully functioning peasant village built on the grounds of Versailles. She would roam the grounds pretending to live the simple life.

116. In 1906, a three-year-old Swiss toddler was given a harsh sentence for petty theft. When he admitted to the act, he was convicted to three and a half months in prison.

117. Thousands of people attended Andrew Jackson's funeral in 1845, including his pet parrot that was removed for allegedly swearing too much.

118. Hat making in the past involved extended exposure to mercury vapors, which caused poisoning. Symptoms included a lack of coordination and vision along with hearing and speech impairment. This inspired the phrase "Mad as a hatter" and of course, the Mad Hatter of *Alice in Wonderland.*

119. Leonardo da Vinci could write with one hand and draw with the other... simultaneously!

120. According to a receipt for an executioner from France in 1386, a pig was executed by public hanging for the murder of a child. He was provided human clothing for the trial.

121. On Good Friday in 1930, the BBC reported, "There is no news." Instead, they played piano music for the remainder of the 15-minute news segment.

122. Alexander the Great knew how to throw a party. He once held a drinking contest in 324 B.C. among his soldiers. When it was over, 42 people had died from alcohol poisoning. The winner, a Greek soldier named Promachus, consumed the equivalent of 13-liters of unmixed wine and died four days later from alcohol poisoning.

123. In 1999, Furbies were banned from the National Security Agency's headquarters and were branded a threat to national security along with arms traders and drug smugglers. It was feared the toys might repeat secrets of national security.

124. The Catholic Church once put a dead Pope on trial. After Pope Formosus died in 896 A.D., his successor had his remains exhumed, dressed in papal robes and put on trial for a long list of political charges. The corpse was found guilty.

125. Purple is often referred to as a 'royal' color. For centuries, they relied only on natural dyes until synthetics hit the market in 1850. Purple came from a species of sea snails and was the hardest dye to extract and produce. It was so exceedingly rare that it became worth its weight in gold. Only royalty could afford it.

126. A Byzantine historian recorded that in 536 A.D., there was a worldwide dust cloud that blocked out the sun for a year, resulting in widespread famine and disease.

127. The eruption of Krakatoain in 1883 was the loudest sound in recorded history, heard 3,000 miles away. It caused over 36,000 deaths.

128. Mexican General Santa Anna had an elaborate state funeral for his amputated leg.

129. Ice Age Britons were not known for their manners... or people skills. Not only did they indulge in cannibalism, they used human skulls as cups for drinking.

130. The Black Death reduced the population by up to two thirds. In four years, nearly 50 million people died.

131. The great conqueror, Attila the Hun, did not die in the way you might guess for a warrior and military leader. He met his fate by the hand of ... a nosebleed.

132. On May 30th of 1883, during the opening week of the Brooklyn Bridge, a woman tripped. It sparked panic that the bridge was collapsing, resulting in a fatal stampede that ended with 12 people dead and more than 35 wounded.

133. In the 1800s, people bought mummies and held "mummy unwrapping" parties. The fascination with Ancient Egypt became all the rage and was referred to as "Egyptomania".

134. The first car accident occurred in 1891, in Ohio.

135. In 1894, London and New York were "drowning" in horse manure. The Times newspaper predicted that within 50 years, London streets would be buried in 9-feet of poop and horse carcasses. Luckily, the invention of the automobile resolved the problem.

136. The electric chair was invented by a dentist.

137. In the 19th century, a popular medicine used to alleviate pain in infants, "Mrs. Winslow's Soothing Syrup," included morphine and alcohol. It is no surprise that it took the pain away!

138. Abraham Lincoln's dog, Fido, was also assassinated.

139. How's this for health insurance? Ancient Chinese doctors could only receive payment if the patient was cured.

140. Cleopatra was the product of incest and continued the family tradition by marrying two of her brothers.

141. We've heard the saying, "Pain is beauty", but not "life threatening"! Infamous 18th century rivals, Kitty Fisher and Maria Gunning, both died of lead poisoning by excessive use of make-up. At the time, make-up contained lead.

142. In Germany, around 1923, banknotes had lost so much value due to hyperinflation that they were used as wallpaper.

143. Lord Byron kept a pet bear in his Trinity College dorm room. He was told that dogs were strictly banned from the campus, so he brought along a different furry friend.

144. The Woolly Mammoth roamed the Earth when the Egyptian Pyramids were being built.

145. More than 8,100 U.S. troops are still listed as missing in action from the Korean War.

146. Hitler, Mussolini and Stalin were all nominated for Nobel Peace Prize. Of course, they were not awarded the honor... for obvious reasons.

147. During World War II, two Polish doctors saved the lives of over 8,000 Jews by faking a typhoid outbreak. They stopped Nazi forces by entering 12 towns with this claim.

148. The Democratic donkey symbol was adopted in 1828, when Andrew Jackson's opponents called him a "jackass". The elephant symbol for the Republic Party was appointed after a satirical cartoon labeling an elephant "the Republican vote".

149. Theodore Roosevelt was the first president to call his residence in Washington, D.C. the "White House." Prior to his term, it had been called the "Executive Mansion" or the "President's House".

150. Have you ever wondered how the wild animals got into the Colosseum? The Roman Imperial army created specialized fighting units to capture dangerous wild animals from Africa and Asia to fight in the Colosseum. They were forbidden from harming the animals and were considered to have one of the most dangerous jobs in the empire.

151. There are at least 50 warheads and 9 nuclear reactors lost at sea since 1956.

152. The current 50-star flag of the United States was designed by a 17-year-old as a school project. He received a B-, but was told the teacher would reconsider if Congress accepted the subpar design. That's exactly what happened and his grade was changed to an A.

153. Peter the Great was not the most forgiving man. He executed his wife's lover, then forced her to keep her lover's head in a jar of alcohol in her bedroom.

154. Don't mess with dad. In early Rome, a father could legally kill anyone in his family.

155. During the first battle of the American Civil War, hundreds of civilians from Washington D.C. were so confident that the Union would win that they came to watch the battle. They even brought picnic baskets. When the Union lost, the civilians were caught in the retreat of the Northern army.

156. Due to climate abnormalities, 1816 was called "The Year Without a Summer". Evidence suggests that it was largely due to the eruption of Mount Tambora in the Dutch East Indies. But some good did come of it: the grey skies and rainfall in Switzerland drove Mary Shelley to stay indoors, where she wrote *Frankenstein*.

157. The world's first traffic signal did not work out so well. Installed in London in 1868, it exploded less than a month later, badly injuring the policeman operating it.

158. Dr. Seuss made a bet with his publisher that he could complete a book with only 50 words. He won. That book is titled, *Green Eggs and Ham*.

159. It's always a challenge finding the right firmness in a pillow. Ancient Egyptians weren't so picky. They used slabs of stones as pillows.

160. Have you noticed a cigar in Winston Churchill's mouth in many of his photos? That's because he smoked 15 cigars a day!

161. Prior to the 1960s, tobacco companies ran physician-endorsed ads suggesting that smoking had health benefits.

162. Saddam Hussein was awarded the key to the city of Detroit in 1980.

163. Martin Luther King Junior's "I Have a Dream" speech in 1963 is considered one of the greatest in American history. Many do not know that he pushed aside his notes and improvised some of his most iconic lines.

164. By the end of World War I, the American military had diagnosed almost 400,000 cases of syphilis and gonorrhea, a historic high.

165. In the early days of the modern Olympic Games, medals were awarded for art.

166. In order to begin construction on the Niagara Falls Suspension Bridge in 1848, engineers needed to secure a line across the 800-foot chasm. It was far too dangerous to do so from the water, so the lead engineer held a kite-flying contest. The winner, a young local boy, was paid $5 for securing the first line over the river.

167. English was once a language for "commoners". The British elites spoke French.

168. The longest war in history was between the Netherlands and the Isles of Scilly. It lasted 335 years, from 1651 to 1986. There were no casualties.

169. In 1856, Abraham Lincoln delivered a speech so captivating that each and every reporter present forgot to take notes. It is believed that the content was a passionate condemnation of slavery, but we can only guess. It is known as "Lincoln's Lost Speech".

170. The time span between the Stegosaurus and the Tyrannosaurus Rex is larger than the span between the Tyrannosaurus Rex and you!

171. Kissing after we say "I Do" is not purely out of romance. When ancient Romans reached an agreement, they would kiss to legally seal the contract. The practice was used in marriage contract as well, which has continued into modern times.

172. The world's first recorded speeding ticket was given to Walter Arnold in Kent for going four times the speed limit... at 8 miles per hour.

173. A scientist who helped develop the atomic bomb ended up winning a Nobel peace prize 50 years later after leading a campaign to eliminate nuclear weapons.

174. Nail polish originated in China as early as 3000 B.C. In ancient Egypt, women used nail color to signify social class rank. A reddish brown was worn by the upper class using henna, while women of lower class could only use pale colors.

175. The ancient Greeks and Romans believed that diamonds were tears cried by the gods or particles from falling stars. The early association between diamonds and romance may have started when Romans believed that Cupid's arrows were tipped with diamonds.

176. While George W. Bush was the target of several assassination attempts and plots, his closest call was by a man named Vladimir Arutyunian. In 2005, Vladimir threw a grenade at the President. The grenade was live and the pin had been pulled, but it did not explode.

177. During the early 1800s, the name Mary was so popular that nearly half the women in U.K. shared that name.

178. Franklin D. Roosevelt was the first president to name a woman to his cabinet.

179. In 1847, Dr. Robert Liston performed an amputation in 25 seconds. He operated so quickly that he accidentally amputated his assistant's fingers as well. Both later died of sepsis, along with a spectator who reportedly died of shock. This resulted in the only known procedure with a 300% mortality rate.

180. The first American automobile race was held in Chicago in 1895 between 6 cars. The winning car's average speed was a whopping 7 miles per hour.

181. You would think this rumor was started by a 5th grader: In the 18th century many prominent voices were concerned by an "epidemic" affecting young people who were spending too much time reading books. It was diagnosed as "a dangerous disease".

182. During the Great Depression, people could not afford new clothes, so they would make them out of flour sacks. Distributors decided to make their sacks more colorful and even patterned to help the population remain somewhat fashionable and boost sales.

183. There is no evidence that Viking helmets ever had horns.

184. We should all thank our dentists today. In early dentistry, teeth were pulled from the mouths of dead soldiers for use as prosthetics.

185. 1.7 billion years ago, there was a natural nuclear reactor that ran for a few hundred thousand years.

186. The first high heeled shoes were worn by Egyptian butchers to help them walk above the bloodied bodies of animal carcasses.

187. The record for the most flowers sold in one day in U.S. history was the day after Elvis Presley died in 1977. Memphis ran out of flowers and scrambled to get additional flowers shipped in from around the nation.

188. Between 1798 and the Civil War, the U.S. Navy lost two-thirds as many officers to dueling as it did to more than 60 years of combat at sea.

189. Apparently, there was an early form of Yelp. The world's oldest known complaint letter was written to a Sumerian copper merchant on a clay tablet almost 4,000 years ago. It read: "You put ingots which were not good before my messenger and said, 'If you want to take them, take them; if you do not want to take them, go away!'" Needless to say, he was an unhappy customer.

190. It took scholars more than two decades to decipher The Rosetta Stone. While scholars were able to quickly translate the 54 lines of Greek and 32 lines of demotic inscribed on the stone, fully deciphering the 14 lines of hieroglyphics took years.

191. In the 1920s, before alarm clocks were invented, there was a profession called a "knocker-up". It involved going from client to client tapping on their windows and banging on their door with long sticks until they were awoken.

192. It became illegal to sell ice-cream sodas on a Sunday in the American town of Evanston during the late 19th century. To get around the problem some traders replaced the soda with syrup and called the dessert an "Ice Cream Sunday." Today, we cherish them as "Sundaes".

193. Ancient Romans committed a faux pas in today's fashion. They wore socks with sandals.

194. Jack the Ripper only killed on the weekends in the early morning hours. All five victims were killed on a Friday, Saturday or Sunday.

195. In English gambling dens in the 18th century, a person was hired solely to swallow the dice in the event of a police raid.

196. Many consider the wheel to be the first big invention, but it was actually invented thousands of years after boats, woven cloth, sewing needles, rope and even the flute.

197. No one will ever rank higher in the U.S. Military than George Washington.

198. Neil Armstrong's NASA application was almost rejected for being late.

199. During the Boston Tea Party, 342 chests of tea were thrown into the Harbor.

200. JFK, Aldous Huxley, and C.S. Lewis all died on the same day.

Food

201. Nowadays, sweet tea is sold at almost every fast-food restaurant for a steal. However, southern sweet tea was originally used to display wealth. Tea, ice, and sugar were all very expensive at the time.

202. It's estimated that the New York Harbor once was home to half of the world's oyster supply. Ellis Island and Liberty Island were known as Little Oyster and Big Oyster, respectively, because of that.

203. Lobster wasn't always such a delicacy. In the 1800s, feeding lobster to prisoners was considered cruel and unusual punishment. Lobsters were referred to as the "cockroaches of the sea".

204. Imagine trying to make a sandwich in space. It would take two people! For this reason, NASA has used flour tortillas in space shuttles since the 1980s.

205. Boston is home to The Union Oyster House, the oldest continuously operating restaurant in the United States, which opened in 1826.

206. The holes in Swiss cheese, known as eyes, have been a source of aggravation in the past for commercial cheese slicers. In 2000, the FDA regulated the holes in Swiss cheese to be between 3/8 and 13/16 of an inch in diameter.

207. Flamingo tongues were an ancient Roman delicacy.

208. Ruth Graves Wakefield invented the chocolate chip cookie around 1938. She sold her recipe to Nestle for one dollar and a lifetime supply of chocolate.

209. Pound cake got its name from its original recipe, which called for a pound each of butter, eggs, sugar, and flour.

210. A janitor at the Frito-Lay plant invented Flamin' Hot Cheetos. He is now an Executive at PepsiCo North America.

211. Figs depend on wasps to make their seeds and distribute their pollen. In turn, the fig tree acts as a womb where the fig wasps can reproduce.

212. Nearly all varieties of corn have an even number of rows.

213. Baby carrots were invented almost by accident, when a farmer got sick of throwing away his damaged and misshapen carrots.

214. Most wasabi consumed is just colored horseradish.

215. Don't be fooled. Store bought 100% "real" orange juice is 100% artificially flavored.

216. The most expensive pizza in the world comes from Salerno, Italy and costs $12,000. It takes 72 hours to make.

217. Vanilla is the second most expensive spice in the world (after saffron) because its production is so labor-intensive.

218. When you shake a can of mixed nuts, the larger nuts will rise to the top.

219. Strawberries contain more vitamin C than oranges.

220. Ben Cohen, one of the founders and tasters of Ben & Jerry's suffers from a condition called anosmia limiting his sense of smell. This is the reason why their ice cream is so rich and contains other sensory features such as colors and textures.

221. Olive oil counterfeiting is a big issue in Italy. Many imported bottles actually don't live up to their "extra virgin" claim. The business has been corrupted by the Mafia, which makes an estimated 16 billion dollars a year in tampering with Italian food products!

222. It's not your fault that you crave chocolate. Blame your primate ancestors. Humans are born craving sugar. Millions and millions of years ago, apes survived on sugar-rich fruit. These animals evolved to like riper fruit because it had a higher sugar content than unripe fruit and therefore supplied more energy.

223. Coconut water can be used as blood plasma in emergency situations.

224. The phrase, "You're a real peach" originated from the tradition of giving peaches to loved ones.

225. The most American of condiments, Ketchup, isn't even American. It's Asian.

226. Doritos were invented at Disneyland.

227. You are 99.9% genetically similar to the person next to you. You also share 60% of your DNA with a banana.

228. Potatoes have more chromosomes than humans. Humans have 46, potatoes have 48.

229. The Lollipop was named after one of the most famous racehorses in the early 1900s, Lolly Pop.

230. Cooking was once considered the woman's job, but today there are more men in the culinary profession than women.

231. Canola oil was originally called rapeseed oil, but rechristened by the Canadian oil industry in 1978. "Canola" is short for "Canadian Oil, Low Acid."

232. Onion is Latin for "large pearl." Onions, with their ringed layers, represented eternity and were found in the eyes of King Ramses IV who died in 1160 B.C.

233. Kale is all the rage these days, but before 2013 the biggest buyer of kale is not who you would expect... it was Pizza Hut. They used kale as a decorative garnish for their salad bars.

234. The vintage date on a bottle of wine indicates the year the grapes were harvested, not the year of bottling.

235. Americans eat three pounds of peanut butter per person every year. That's enough peanut butter to coat the floor of the Grand Canyon!

236. Some people swear that you can save a corked bottle of wine with just a penny... literally! Drop a clean penny in the glass of wine and swirl it around. When you remove it, the wine should taste much better.

237. The difference between apple juice and apple cider is that the juice is pasteurized and the cider is not. It takes about a third of a bushel of apples to make one gallon of cider.

238. The popsicle was accidentally invented by an 11-year-old in 1905. He mixed sugary soda powder with water and left it out overnight. It was a cold evening, so the mixture froze. He woke up to the discovery and devoured the icy treat by licking it off the wooden stirrer.

239. The reason why peppers taste hot is because of a chemical compound called capsaicin. When you bite into your nachos and hit a jalapeño, the chemical binds to your sensory nerves and tricks them into thinking your mouth is actually being burned. The hottest pepper in the world is fittingly called "dragon's breath".

240. Almonds aren't actually nuts at all. They are the seeds of a flower and are directly related to the botanical families of orchids and roses.

241. The inner part of bread surrounded by the crust is called the "crumb". That is why small bits of this part of the bread are referred to as "crumbs".

242. Tired of shedding tears over a silly onion? Stick it in the freezer for 15 minutes prior to cutting. The cold inhibits the release of eye-irritating chemicals.

243. There is an average of 200 tiny seeds on every strawberry. They are the only fruit with seeds that grow on the outside.

244. Coffee may have been discovered by a goat. There is a popular Ethiopian legend that tells the story of a goat herder finding his goats frolicking and full of energy after eating from a coffee shrub. He tried it for himself and discovered the same effect.

245. There are approximately 350 different pasta shapes around the world. Italians will tell you that each shape and size serves a different culinary purpose. Do you research before preparing your next bowl of pasta!

246. When a cranberry is ripe, it will bounce like a rubber ball.

247. A cluster of bananas is called a "hand". A single banana is justly called a "finger".

248. In Ancient Rome, a soldier's pay consisted in part of salt. It became known as solarium argentum then, or "salary" as we call it today.

249. It is against the law to put pretzels in bags in Philadelphia.

250. Potato chips were invented in response to a customer complaint. Chef George Crum had a customer complain that his potatoes were too thick and soggy. Incredibly frustrated,

George cut them as thinly as possible, fried them until they were crispy and sent them back to the customer.

251. The first food ever to be microwaved was popcorn. Great idea! The second was an egg which exploded in the face of the experimenter. Not such a great idea.

252. There are over 87,000 drink combinations at Starbucks!

253. Baskin-Robbins once made ketchup-flavored ice cream for a friend who put ketchup on everything.

254. Mongolians invented lemonade around 1299 A.D.

255. Gatorade was invented by the University of Florida's physicians to fight player fatigue for one specific team: The Florida Gators.

256. Legend has it that sandwiches were invented in 1762 so that the Earl of Sandwich could keep gambling. His cook put some beef between two slices bread and the rest is history. Today, Americans eat more than 300 million sandwiches a day.

257. German Chocolate Cake doesn't hail from Germany. In 1852, a Texas woman sent in a cake recipe to a Dallas newspaper using "Baker's German Sweet Chocolate" baking bar. The recipe, known as "German's Chocolate Cake" was so popular that sales for the chocolate bar spiked. Somewhere along the way the apostrophe and "s" was dropped.

258. You burn about 20 calories per hour chewing gum.

259. You have heard that chicken soup is good for the soul, but it was once considered an aphrodisiac in the Middle Ages.

260. Children may claim to fear vegetables to avoid them, but the actual fear of vegetables is called lachanophobia.

261. An 18-ounce jar of peanut butter contains about 850 peanuts.

262. The M's in M & M's stand for Mars & Murrie, the co-creators of the candy. The chocolates debuted in 1941 and were invented as a means for soldiers to enjoy chocolate without it melting in their hands.

263. Ben and Jerry's receives about 13,000 flavor suggestions a year. They read them all.

264. Waffle cones were invented at the World's Fair in 1904 when an ice cream vendor ran out of dishes. He enlisted the help from the waffle pastry vendor next door to create a new "dish".

265. Carmine, a food dye used in many bright red food products, is manufactured from an insect called the cochineal.

266. Refried beans are only fried once. The reason for this misconception is a translation error. Frijoles refritos actually translates as "well fried beans".

267. Canned food was invented in 1810, but the can opener did not come for another 45 years. Canned food would come with instructions to "cut around the top near the outer edge with a chisel and hammer".

268. Honey is the only food with an (almost) eternal shelf life. It will not rot and it can last up to 3000 years. Modern archeologists, excavating ancient Egyptian tombs, have often found pots of honey, thousands of years old, perfectly preserved.

269. The phrase "breakfast is the most important meal of the day" came from a 1944 marketing campaign to sell more cereal. The editor was John Harvey Kellogg, co-inventor of the flaked   cereal.

270. The number of jars of Nutella sold in a year could cover The Great Wall of China eight times. Sounds like a delicious idea!

271. Hawaii is the only place in the United States where coffee is grown commercially. It is the only state that meets the proper growing conditions of high altitudes, tropical climates and rich soil.

272. Eating poppy seed bread before a drug test can get you fired. Testing can rule out heroin, but not other opiates.

273. Twinkies were originally filled with banana cream and were sold that way for years. It wasn't until a banana shortage during World War II that the company was forced to switch to the vanilla-cream filling that we know and love today.

274. You cannot taste food until it is mixed with saliva.

275. Mangoes can get a sunburn.

276. Croissants are not a French food, they're Austrian.

277. Grossed out by your in-flight meal? It may be due to the preparation, but we can't blame it all on the chef. In the air, our sense of smell and taste decrease from 20 to 50 percent. That's the equivalent of having a bad cold.

278. The "overbite" dates back to the adoption of the table knife and fork about 250 years ago. When we started cutting food into small portions, our jaws changed. In China, the overbite emerged about 900 years sooner with the invention of chopsticks.

279. Meat was so plentiful on the Lewis and Clark expedition that each man ate about 9 pounds of meat a day!

280. The largest restaurant, Damascus Gate, is in Syria and has 6,014 seats.

281. In 2016, a street food vendor in Singapore was awarded a Michelin star.

282. In Britain, there was a lawsuit that took place trying to prove that Pringles are not *really* potato chips because they do not have enough potato content.

283. Cheese is the most stolen food in the world.

284. Although Italy is synonymous with tomato sauces, Italian chefs didn't start cooking with the tomato until the 16th century. In the early 1500s when tomatoes were first imported, they were thought to be poisonous and were used solely as decoration.

285. In 2012, divers discovered a 2,000-year-old Roman shipwreck off the coast of Italy that was so well preserved even the food was intact in its storage jars.

286. Aunt Jemima pancake flour, invented in 1889, was the first ready-mix food to be sold commercially.

287. Wint-O-Green Lifesavers will spark when you bite them in the dark. It is a miniaturized version of lighting.

288. Tiramisu means "pick me up" or "cheer me up" in Italian.

289. We don't often think of yogurt as spoiled milk, but that's exactly what it is. Many historians attribute yogurt to Central Asia around 6,000 B.C. as a result of storing milk by primitive methods in warm climates.

290. The beloved Pez candies were marketed more than 70 years ago in Vienna as a cigarette substitute. It obtained its name from the German word for Peppermint, **PfeffErmiZ**.

291. Surprisingly, the cotton candy machine was invented in 1897, by a dentist. However, cotton candy isn't a modern invention. It dates back to the 15th century when Italian cooks spun sugar then draped it around wooden broom handles to create sculptures.

292. The term 'soft drink' was first used to describe drinks without alcohol. However, Russia did not consider beer to be alcohol until 2011. It was previously considered a soft drink.

293. Casu marzu is a traditional Sardinian sheep milk cheese that contains live maggots inside.

294. Popcorn isn't the most popular movie snack everywhere. In Colombia, dried ants are a popular alternative, while Korean moviegoers enjoy snacking on a bag of dried cuttlefish.

295. The World Health Organization has classified processed meats, including ham, salami, sausages and hot dogs, as a Group 1 carcinogen.

296. No fridge? No problem, if you have a frog handy! Before refrigerators were invented, Russians and Finns would put live frogs in their milk to preserve it. Frogs have peptides in their skin that kill bacteria.

297. Banana "trees" are actually giant herbs. Their trunks are not made of wood, but tightened leaves.

298. In addition to the 14 chemicals thrown into the mix when making McDonald's French fries, they are sugar coated before being fried to ensure a golden color.

299. It is estimated that the average child will eat 1,500 Peanut Butter and Jelly sandwiches by high school graduation.

300. The creator of Tabasco, Edmund McIlhenny, was a big fan of reusing and recycling. He originally packaged his hot sauce in used cologne bottles.

Celebrity

301. Elvis Presley was a natural blonde. He starting dying his hair in high school.

302. Leonardo DiCaprio was named after Leonardo da Vinci. While in Florence, Italy, his pregnant mother felt him kick while she was in standing in front of a da Vinci painting at the Uffizi Gallery.

303. Chris Kirkpatrick founded 'N Sync after he didn't make the cut with the Backstreet Boys. AJ beat him out of the spot, but it all worked out in the end!

304. Sara Jessica Parker is a descendant of someone who was accused of being a witch in the Salem Witch Trials. Ironically, she played a Salem Witch in *Hocus Pocus*.

305. Christopher Walken traveled with the circus when he was 15 as a lion tamer.

306. When Madonna moved to New York City, she was strapped for cash and took a job at Dunkin' Donuts in Times Square. She got fired on the first day because she squirted jelly on a customer.

307. Steve Buscemi was a New York City firefighter from 1980 to 1984.

308. A Baltimore TV producer told Oprah Winfrey that she was "unfit for television news."

309. Sean Connery wore a toupee in every James Bond movie he appeared in.

310. Before he started his famous daytime talk show, Jerry Springer was the mayor of Cincinnati!

311. Sex guru Dr. Ruth is a trained Israeli sniper.

312. Natalie Portman is a Harvard graduate who has been published in two scientific journals.

313. On a long list of bizarre purchases, Nicolas Cage once bought a pet octopus for $150,000. He also bought shrunken pygmy heads and a nine-foot-tall burial tomb.

314. Bill Murray's 20th birthday was not so great. He was arrested at a Chicago airport for trying to smuggle two-pound "bricks" of marijuana onto a plane. It was worth $20,000 at the time (almost six times that today)!

315. Simon Cowell got his start as a runner on Stanley Kubrick's horror classic, *The Shining*. He polished the axe used by Jack Nicholson to bust through the door.

316. Robert Downey Jr. claims that Burger King saved him from his drug addiction. He was so disgusted by the burger he ordered that he tossed the food along with all of his drugs into the ocean to clean up his act immediately.

317. Steve Jobs used to relieve stress by soaking his feet in Apple's company toilets.

318. Uma Thurman's dad was the first Westerner ever to become a Tibetan Buddhist monk.

319. James Cameron, the famous director of epic movies like *Titanic* and *Avatar*, dropped out of college to drive a truck. The money he made supported his film career and his time spent on the road helped him brainstorm screenplay ideas.

320. Julie Andrews' singing voice was almost entirely ruined by a botched surgery in 1997.

321. Walt Disney, the man behind Mickey Mouse and "the most magical place on earth", had an intense fear of mice.

322. Barack Obama, Hillary Clinton, and Martin Luther King, Jr. have all won more Grammys than Katy Perry. All three of them have won Grammys in the Spoken Word category.

323. Oona Chaplin (from *Game of Thrones*) is the granddaughter of Charlie Chaplin!

324. Hugh Hefner, founder of *Playboy* magazine, did not lose his virginity until he was 22 years old.

325. When Jim Carrey was just a teenager, he and his entire family took janitorial jobs. He worked 8-hour shifts after school.

326. In 1969, much before Pierce Brosnan rose to fame, he did a fire-eating act at the Oval House.

327. Martin Luther King Jr. died when he was 39 years old. According to Taylor Branch, his autopsy found that he had the heart of a 60-year-old from stress.

328. During World War II, Audrey Hepburn was a courier for resistance fighters in Holland. Children were often give this work because the Nazi's were unlikely to search them.

329. Emily Blunt had a stutter until the age of 14. She claims that it was acting that cured her of it.

330. Everyone knows that Jackie Chan does his own stunts...even the insurance companies. He and his stunt team have tremendous difficulty getting insured in the U.S. and Jackie Chan will pay for his team's injuries out of pocket.

331. A newspaper editor fired Walt Disney because he lacked creativity.

332. J.K. Rowling was fired from her job as a secretary for daydreaming too much. Her severance check helped her support her writing career.

333. Arnold Schwarzenegger first picked up a barbell at the age of 13 and chose bodybuilding as a career at the age of 14.

334. Jaleel White, well-known for his role as Steve Urkel in *Family Matters*, provided the voice of Sonic the Hedgehog.

335. In 1965, when Goldie Hawn was working in New York City, she was in a car crash on the West Side Highway. The doctor said it was a miracle that she and the other people in the car even survived.

336. Lady Gaga wrote *Born This Way* in 10 minutes flat, calling it "immaculate conception".

337. Ferruccio Lamborghini manufactured tractors when he decided to purchase a Ferrari. He wasn't so impressed by the car and confronted Enzo Ferrari about his frustrations. Ferrari responded by saying that it was the driver, not the car, that was the problem. Lamborghini accepted this as a challenge, not an insult.

338. The Wright Brothers only flew together once, only after gaining their father's permission. They had always promised him that they wouldn't fly together, to avoid a double tragedy if there was an accident.

339. Adele has to have her social media posts approved by two people before sharing. Apparently, she sent out a few too many drunk tweets and lost the privilege!

340. Two-time Academy Award winner, Hilary Swank, lived out of a car until her mother saved enough money to rent an apartment. She calls her mother the inspiration for her acting career.

341. John Cena, WWE superstar, has granted more than 500 Make-a-Wish requests. That's more than anyone in the charity's history. After the 500th, he said he would "drop everything" to do it again.

342. Gwyneth Paltrow had a minor role in the 1991 film, *Hook*. She played the young Wendy Darling in the flashback scenes.

343. The author of *Jaws* wished he never wrote it. He dedicated the last decade of his life to the preservation of sharks to make up for the mass hysteria he created for portraying them as killing machines.

344. Shakira speaks 4 languages: Spanish, English, Portuguese and Italian.

345. At the age of 12, Jay Z shot his drug-addicted brother for stealing money from him.

346. OJ Simpson was originally cast to play the title role in *Terminator*, but director James Cameron thought Simpson was "too nice" and did not feel that he would be believable as a killer.

347. Eminem was severely and constantly bullied in public school. So badly that his mother sued the local school board for "failing to sufficiently protect her child".

348. Ryan Gosling was almost in the Backstreet Boys. He was offered a place in the boy band.

349. Mila Kunis was 14 years old when she auditioned for *That 70s Show*, but the age requirement was 18. She told the casting directors that she would be 18 on her birthday, but never said which birthday.

350. Will Smith can solve a Rubik's Cube in under a minute.

351. *Star Wars* creator George Lucas hired Harrison Ford, then a carpenter, to build a door in the casting offices. The director wasn't just impressed by the star's woodwork skills. Despite hundreds of people competing for the role, Lucas decided Harrison was actually the best person for the part.

352. When Cameron Diaz got the part in *The Mask*, she had no previous acting experience.

353. Martha Stewart was once a fashion model.

354. Joaquin Phoenix spent most of his early childhood travelling around South America, as his parents were part of religious cult, The Children of God. Rose McGowan's parents were a part of the same cult and at the age of 15, she emancipated herself from them.

355. Woody Harrelson's dad was a hitman who murdered a Texas salesman for $1,500.

356. Christian Bale was inspired by Tom Cruise for the mannerisms he used in *American Psycho*. After seeing Tom Cruise on *David Letterman*, Bale noticed that Cruise had a very intense friendliness with nothing behind the eyes.

357. Taylor Swift grew up on a Christmas tree farm.

358. While serving in the United States Army, Mr. T (then Nathaniel Tureaud) was given a punishment of chopping down trees. The sergeant left Turneaud, but did not specify how many to cut down. He returned alarmed to find 70 trees downed in just 3.5 hours.

359. Leighton Meester was born in prison. Her mom was serving time for smuggling drugs.

360. Sylvester Stallone wrote the script for *"Rocky"* and was homeless at the time. A week before he sold the script, he had to sell his dog to make ends meet. He approached the new owners 6-months later and begged them to sell the dog back. They were not thrilled, but obliged. They felt that the dog deserved a place in the movie.

361. For her role in *Winter's Bone*, Jennifer Lawrence learned how to skin squirrels.

362. Matthew McConaughey has a fear of revolving doors. He gets terrified just being near them.

363. Following Marilyn Monroe's death, Joe DiMaggio was so devastated that he delivered flowers to her grave twice a week for over 20 years. He never remarried, and his last words before he died in 1999 were, "I'll finally get to see Marilyn."

364. Jackie Chan's parents were so poor that they had to consider selling him to pay for the $200 hospital bill after he was born through cesarean surgery. His father borrowed the money and ate dog food for two-years to save cash.

365. At the age of 16, Jim Carrey dropped out of high school to help support his family and focus on comedy.

366. Lucille Ball was a pencil hoarder. When she was young, her family was so poor that she could not afford a pencil for school. Since then, she would collect pencils and even had a closet filled with unopened pencil packages.

367. James Lipton was once a pimp in France.

368. Tommy Lee Jones has a long list of questions that he will not answer during interviews. The list includes his marriages, his real estate holdings, his political views and his friendships. Interviewers must choose their questions wisely!

369. While in South Africa for a year in high school, Rebel Wilson contracted malaria and hallucinated that she was an Oscar winning actress. This convinced her to pursue an acting career.

370. Warren Buffett made enough money delivering magazine subscriptions door-to-door to invest in a 40-acre farm in Nebraska by the age of 15.

371. Geena Davis is an archer who made it to the semifinals in the qualification rounds for the 2000 Olympics.

372. None of The Beatles could read music. George Harrison worried that too much music theory would ruin the creativity of the songwriting process.

373. Rihanna was an army cadet that trained with the Barbadian military. Fellow singer Shontelle was her drill sergeant.

374. Elizabeth Taylor was the first actress to be paid $1 million dollars for a role.

375. Judy Garland had become close friends with President John F. Kennedy. He would randomly call her to ask that she sing "Somewhere Over the Rainbow".

376. Whoopi Goldberg chose her stage name not only because of the Whoopee Cushion, but also because her mother thought "Goldberg" was Jewish-sounding enough to make it in Hollywood.

377. Daniel Radcliffe wore the same outfit for 6 months during the run of the West End play *Equus* to make the paparazzi angry. The photos would be rendered useless because it appeared as if they were all taken on the same day.

378. Judy Garland was put on a strict diet and even bullied for her weight while filming *The Wizard of Oz*. She was only 16 years old.

379. Steven Tyler estimates that he spent at least 5-6 million dollars on cocaine in the 70s and 80s.

380. Brad Pitt and Angelina Jolie sold a photo of their newborn twins to *People* and *Hello!* magazines for $14 million. They gave all the money to charity.

381. David Bowie's eye is permanently dilated from a fight he got in when he was 15.

382. Country singer Dolly Parton entered a 'Dolly Parton look-alike contest' but lost to a drag queen. The other contestants didn't know they were going up against the real Dolly.

383. Daniel Radcliffe's stunt double was paralyzed after an explosion on the film set of *Harry Potter and The Deathly Hallows.*

384. When Tupac Shakur was in prison, Jim Carrey would write him funny letters to cheer him up.

385. Jennifer Lopez was homeless as a teen while she began her performing career. She slept on the sofa of her dance studio for months. She was kicked out of the house after fighting with her mother over her career choice.

386. Martha Stewart became a billionaire for the second time while in prison.

387. When Stephen King was 2 years old, his father left the family. He went to "buy a pack of cigarettes" and never came back.

388. Chuck Norris' first name is actually Carlos. His full real name is Carlos Ray.

389. Gwen Stefani has only had three boyfriends in her life. Her short list includes *No Doubt* bandmate Tony Kanal, ex-husband Gavin Rossdale, and current love interest Blake Shelton.

390. Michael Jackson was scheduled to have a meeting in one of the Twin Towers on the morning of 9/11, but missed it because he overslept.

391. Jimmy Carter was the first U.S. president to have been born in a hospital.

392. Lucille Ball was one of the first women to have her pregnancy depicted on air. She and the rest of the cast weren't allowed to say the word "pregnant" on air. CBS thought the word was too vulgar.

393. In 2011, Jolie told *60 Minutes* that she was inspired to become a funeral director due to a deeply scarring family death and how the funeral was handled.

394. For five weeks, Will Ferrell played Santa Claus at a mall in Pasadena, California with friend and future co-star Chris Kattan (who worked as an elf).

395. Charlize Theron was "discovered" when an agent witnessed her in a shouting match at a bank teller who wouldn't cash her check.

396. Louis Armstrong played the trumpet so much that he had enormous callouses on his lips. He had to cut them off with a razor blade.

397. Brandy killed someone in a car accident by failing to brake immediately.

398. Kesha has an IQ of 140 and scored a 1500 on her SATs.

399. Justin Timberlake is the voice of the "I'm Lovin' It" campaign for McDonald's.

400. Frank Oz was the voice of Yoda, Miss Piggy and Cookie Monster.

Sports

401. The Buffalo Bills haven't made the playoffs since 1999, when Bill Clinton was President.

402. Ray Caldwell pitched a complete game after being struck by lightning. He was struck in the middle of the ninth inning and "shook it off".

403. There have been 373 sets of brothers who have played in the NFL and 217 sets of fathers and sons.

404. In 1975, Junko Tabei from Japan became the first woman to reach the top of Everest.

405. The average golf ball has 336 dimples, although they can range between 300 to 500.

406. Shaquille O'Neal missed 5,317 free throws during his NBA career. The foul line was not his greatest talent.

407. There are only 18 minutes of total action during a baseball game. That means the average MLB game is 90% standing around.

408. Live pigeon shooting was an Olympic sport. In the 1900 Olympic Games in Paris, hundreds of pigeons were released in front of competitors. For obvious reasons, this was the first and last time it was included in the Olympics.

409. The two golf balls that Alan Shephard hit on the moon with a six-iron are still there.

410. ☐The Bears, Browns, Giants, Lions, Packers and Steelers are the six NFL franchises without cheerleaders.

411. The Philippines has competed in the most summer Olympics without winning a single gold medal.

412. Russell Erxleben is the highest drafted kicker in NFL history. The New Orleans Saints drafted him 11th overall. He kicked just four field goals before moving to punter.

413. Babe Ruth only won four World Series in 15 seasons with the New York Yankees. Yogi Berra, however, won 10 in 18 seasons, then three more as a coach.

414. The fastest knock out in professional boxing history happened in 10.5 seconds.

415. The Stanley Cup has been through many hands since 1893. Each player on the winning team gets 24-hours with the trophy. Through the years, it has been used as a flower pot, a cereal bowl and an ice cream sundae bowl. It was accidentally left by the side of the road, been to a strip club and tossed into a swimming pool. It was even lost on a 2010 flight from New Jersey to Vancouver. It was later recovered by an Air Canada employee.

416. Princess Ann, the daughter of Queen Elizabeth II, did not have to undergo gender verification at the 1976 Olympics due to "Royal Courtesy". She rode the Queen's horse, Goodwill.

417. NFL referees receive Super Bowl rings.

418. John Isner and Nicholas Mahut played 183 games over 3 days at the 2010 Wimbledon Championships, which beats the previous record of 112 games.

419. When William G. Morgan came up with Volleyball in 1895, he tried to use a basketball, but found it too heavy. He pulled out the basketball's inflatable rubber inside and played with that until a custom ball was created by A.G. Spalding.

420. The Cubs didn't play any night games at home prior to 1988, when lights were installed at the field.

421. Olympic gold medals are actually made mostly of silver. The 1912 Olympic Games were the last to include medals made of solid gold.

422. The fastest slapshot on record is Bobby Hull's, which registered 118 miles per hour.

423. Before the Bulldog became Georgia's now famous mascot, their first unofficial mascot was a goat.

424. Jerry Rice and Brett Favre are the only non-kickers to play in more than 300 games in the NFL.

425. Sammy Sosa has three of the eight 60-home run seasons in baseball history.

426. The longest recorded point in tennis history occurred in a 1984 women's tennis match. It lasted 29 minutes with the ball crossing the net 643 times.

427. Until 1920, pitchers in Major League Baseball were allowed to grease the ball up with as much saliva as they saw fit. When it was outlawed, those "grandfathered in" could continue until they retired.

428. Steve Young is the only left-handed quarterback in the Pro Football Hall of Fame.

429. The phrase winning something "hands down" refers to a jockey who won a race without whipping his horse or pulling the reins.

430. Missouri is credited with establishing the tradition of Homecoming in the United States in 1911, which was then adopted by most colleges and high schools across the country.

431. On MLB's Opening Day in 1907, the New York Giants hosted the Philadelphia Phillies. New York was hit with a snowstorm that left the stadium filled with snow. When the

Giants fell behind by the sixth inning, Giants fans were so unhappy that they started throwing snowballs at the field. The umpires swiftly called the game and a forfeit was called in the Phillies' favor.

432. In order to take allow pitchers to get a better grip, Major League Baseball wipes down each baseball with mud. They have been doing so for over 75 years.

433. The New England Patriots are the only franchise to have scored three touchdowns in less than one minute.

434. Tony Cloninger, a pitcher playing for the Braves in 1966, became the first play in National League history to hit two grand slams in one game.

435. China did not win an Olympic medal until 1984. At the 2008 Beijing games, the Chinese won 100 medals. Apparently, they finally got the hang of it.

436. There have been three Olympic Games in countries that no longer exist.

437. There are only two out of 365 days of the year with no professional sports games (MLB, NBA, NHL, or NFL).

438. Only 9 goalies have scored a combined 11 goals in the history of the NHL.

439. The New York Yankees were not the original team to introduce pinstripes to Major League Baseball uniforms. In 1911, both the New York Giants and Philadelphia Phillies sported pinstripes on uniforms for the very first time.

440. Penn State's official colors were originally black and pink, but the baseball team's uniforms faded to dark blue and white, so the school changed the colors to the blue and white that we know today.

441. The Cleveland Browns are the only team to neither host nor play in a Super Bowl.

442. The 1992 San Diego Chargers are the only one 0-4 team that has ever made the NFL playoffs.

443. Only one city, Detroit, has won three major sports championships in the same year. In 1935, the Lions won the Super Bowl, the Tigers won the World Series and the Red Wings took the Stanley Cup.

444. Mickey Mantle was originally a shortstop, but after making over a hundred mistakes in his last two seasons in the minor league, he was moved to the outfield.

445. The average life span of an MLB baseball is five to seven pitches.

446. The 12th tiebreaker for a division championship in the NFL is a coin flip.

447. Unlike gold Olympic medals, the UFC belt really is made of gold.

448. Gerard Gordeau's 30-second knockout of Telia Tuli at UFC 1 was the first fight in UFC history. A kick from Gordeau sent one of Tuli's teeth flying into the crowd and two more embedded into Gordeau's foot.

449. The average height of elite female gymnasts has dropped from 5-foot-3 to 4-foot-9 in the last 30 years.

450. Dana White never had a professional boxing fight. As of May 2017, his Net Worth was $500 million.

451. Joe Gibbs is the only coach to win the Super Bowl with three different quarterbacks.

452. The beginnings of "mixed martial arts" can be traced back to the ancient Greeks. Invented as a war technique, but also played as an Olympic sport, pankration was a combination of wrestling and boxing. Anything was permitted except biting, eye gouging or attacking the genitals.

453. Because they both lost so many players to WWII military service, the Pittsburgh Steelers and Philadelphia Eagles combined to become the "Steagles" during the 1943 season.

454. Identified by the name "soccer" in the U.S. and "football" elsewhere, the sport's original name is actually "basket-ball." When the game was first created, the first goals were overturned wicker baskets.

455. During his career, Babe Ruth was not so great as a pinch-hitter, his record just 13 hits in 67 at-bats.

456. The earliest documented wrestling match took place in the Eighth century B.C. at the ancient Olympic Games.

457. The commissioner made the controversial decision to play games two days after John F. Kennedy's assassination, after guidance from JFK's press secretary. He said Robert F. Kennedy told him his brother would have wanted the games to go on. None of the games aired due to the constant coverage post-assassination. Just after the first games kicked off, Lee Harvey Oswald was shot in the parking garage of the Dallas police headquarters while JFK's casket was led through the streets of Washington. Rozelle would call playing those games his biggest regret and his successor, Paul Tagliabue did not make the same mistake after 9/11.

458. Royce Gracie still holds the record for most submission wins in the UFC with 11.

459. Soccer was played by prisoners at London's Newgate Prison in the early 1800s. After having their hands cut off for their crimes, prisoners came up with the game using only their feet.

460. In 1996-1997, the Phoenix Suns had a 10-game winning and losing streak in the same season. They lost the first 13 games, but made it to the playoffs with 10 wins once Jason Kidd recovered from his injury.

461. The Rock won the shortest match in WrestleMania history. It lasted six seconds.

462. Charles Barkley was cut from the basketball team freshman and sophomore year of high school.

463. Contrary to belief, soccer balls are not actually round. They have a slightly oval shape, but the checkered pattern creates the illusion that it is spherical.

464. With a viewership of over 33 million, Hulk Hogan and Andre the Giant's 1988 rematch at The Main Event is currently the most watched wrestling match ever in North American history.

465. There are 32 panels on a traditional soccer ball, one for each country in Europe.

466. In 1841, 9-pin bowling was illegal in Connecticut because it was considered a source of gambling. 10-pin bowling was created to get around the law.

467. The national sport of Canada is soccer, not hockey.

468. "Knickerbockers" in New York is the first indoor bowling alley, built in 1840.

469. In 1965, the average minimum salary in Major League Baseball was just $6,000. This low wage forced many players to work other jobs during the offseason. The minimum salary for the 2017 season is $535,000.

470. The largest loss in any season opener, regardless of location, is 46 points. It occurred in 1987 when the Clippers lost to Nuggets.

471. In Ancient Greek culture, the god, Apollo, was regarded as the inventor and guardian of the sport of boxing.

472. Archie Moore holds the record for most knockouts during a career with 131. He is the only fighter to have faced both Muhammad Ali and Rocky Marciano.

473. King Edward III allegedly outlawed bowling in 1366, so that his troops would stay focused on practicing archery.

474. Greenland is unable to join FIFA because not enough grass grows there for a soccer field. Due to challenging weather conditions, soccer can only be played four months out of the year.

475. Studies show that bare-knuckle fighting may be safer than boxing with gloves. In 100 years of bare-knuckle fighting in the United States, there wasn't a single ring fatality. Today, there are three or four a year.

476. The longest winning street in MMA history was between January 1996 and May 2000, Igor Vovchanchyn won 32 consecutive fights.

477. There have been games played on every day of the week in the modern NFL. The Tuesday game was due to a Pennsylvania blizzard. The Wednesday game was pulled up from Thursday night season opener so it wouldn't overlap with John McCain's speech at the Republican convention. The Friday games were due to Christmas or New Year's.

478. The richest American racehorse of all time is California Chrome. His career earnings total $14,502,650 as of 2017, topping the all-time list for the U.S. and North America.

479. The game of rugby is said to have been invented at Rugby School in 1823, when William Webb Ellis caught the ball and ran with it in a soccer game.

480. At more than 300 revolutions per minute, figure skaters experience as much RPM as astronauts in centrifuge training.

481. The whistle used for the opening match at every Rugby World Cup is the one used by Welsh referee Gil Evans for an England-New Zealand match in 1905.

482. Theodore Roosevelt did more than fight for American conservation. He wrestled, boxed and practiced judo most of his life. He was the first American to earn his brown belt.

483. In 1983, during a game between the New York Yankees and Toronto Blue Jays in Toronto, Yankees right fielder Dave Winfield was warming up when he threw a ball that struck and killed a seagull. Police officials in Toronto arrested Winfield and charged him with cruelty to animals.

484. Kobe Bryant wasn't a Top-10 pick. He was 13th.

485. Twelve horses have won racing's Triple Crown.

486. Secretariat, the Triple Crown winning horse of 1973, was such a star that he was the only non-human on ESPN's 100 Greatest Athletes of the Twentieth Century.

487. Dale Earnhardt died in an accident on the last lap of the Daytona 500 on February 18, 2001. There has not been a death in NASCAR's top series since then.

488. Richard Petty has the most wins in NASCAR history. His 200 wins make up eight percent of all NASCAR wins.

489. Lacrosse is referred to as the fastest sport on two feet.

490. The best American skaters were on route to a competition in Prague in 1961 when their plane crashed, killing everyone on board. The competition was canceled out of respect for the lives lost.

491. Watch your fingers! Male skaters weighing 150 pounds or more can land on the ice following a jump with extraordinary force: more than 1000 lbs. of pressure.

492. In 2003, the World Record for the most spins a figure skater has completed on one foot without stopping is 115.

493. The first recorded downhill skiing race was held in Sweden, in 1879. Alpine skiing as a sport made its Winter Olympic debut in the year 1936.

494. Ancient carvings discovered by archeologists in Norway suggest the locals started skiing many thousands of years ago, with one rock drawing thought to date from 4,500BC.

495. The current world record for the fastest skier is held by Simone Origone of Italy at an incredible 156.2 miles an hour!

496. According to many competitive skiers, the course at Kitzbühel in Tyrol, Austria is the most challenging slope in the world.

497. The fastest recorded speed a person has ever gone on a bike is 167.043 miles per hour.

498. In the early 1900s, 6-day long bicycle races were popular. The winner would be whoever rode the greatest distance in the 6-days. As you can imagine, they would get extremely little sleep and often hallucinate on the track

499. The Tour de France is one of the most famous bicycle races in the world. Since its establishment in 1903, it is considered to be the biggest test of endurance out of all sports. The race includes 21 stages and covers 3,540 kilometers.

500. In 2012, The International Cycling Union announced that no one would be declared the winner of the Tour de France from 1999-2005, after Armstrong was stripped of his titles.

The Human Body

501. Your body is made of about 7 octillion atoms.

502. Your mouth produces about one liter of saliva each day.

503. The largest cell in the human body is the female egg and the smallest is the male sperm.

504. Stomach acid can dissolve metal.

505. Your eyes are always the same size from birth, but your nose and ears never stop growing.

506. Your skin's outer layer sheds every 2-4 weeks, amounting to roughly .07 kilograms of dead skin in a year.

507. While the brain is the tool we use to detect pain, the brain itself cannot feel pain.

508. The notion that we only use ten percent of our brain is untrue. We use virtually every part of our brain and most of it is active almost all of the time.

509. While the four major blood types are most common, there are actually 29 recognized blood groups! One of the rarest is the Bombay blood group, which is found in tribal populations of India.

510. Your brain is sometimes more active when you're asleep than when you're awake.

511. Cells in the inner lens of the eye, muscle cells of the heart, and the neurons of the cerebral cortex are the only cells that will be with you for the entirety of your life.

512. One square centimeter of your skin contains around a hundred pain sensors.

513. The heart has its own electrical supply and will continue to beat when outside the body.

514. Laid end to end, an adult's blood vessels could circle Earth's equator four times!

515. If you were to spread out all the wrinkles in your brain, it would be about the size of a pillowcase.

516. When you were born, you had 300 bones. As an adult, you have 206. Don't worry, the other bones have not disappeared, they have merely fused together.

517. Believe someone when they tell you that you look radiant. Bodies actually give off a tiny amount of light that's too weak for the eye to see!

518. The word "muscle" comes from Latin term meaning "little mouse", which is what Ancient Romans thought flexed bicep muscles resembled.

519. You spend 10 percent of the day blinking.

520. Before the invention of the stethoscope, doctors had to press their ears directly on each patient's chest.

521. Your eyes can distinguish between 2.3 and 7.5 million different colors.

522. They may cry constantly, but babies don't shed tears until they're at least one month old.

523. Your nose can differentiate between 1 trillion different smells.

524. Evidence of heart disease has been found in 3,000-year-old mummies.

525. Your skull is made up of 29 different bones.

526. Your blood makes up about eight percent of your body weight.

527. Teeth are the only part of the human body which cannot heal themselves.

528. A newborn child can breathe and swallow at the same time for up to seven months.

529. When you look at an object, the image of that object appears upside down on your retina. Your brain automatically corrects for this, allowing you to perceive the object the right side up.

530. Humans are the only species that produce emotional tears.

531. Every cell in the body gets blood from the heart except for the corneas.

532. Heart cancer is extremely rare because heart cells stop dividing in early life.

533. A man named Charles Osborne hiccupped for a total of 68 years.

534. Your pinky finger is small, but mighty. Without it, you would lose 50% of your hand's strength.

535. A single human brain generates more electrical impulses in a day than all the telephones of the world combined.

536. A fetus acquires fingerprints at the age of three months.

537. Your heart beats 100,000 times per day, pumping 5.5 litres per minute, which adds up to about 3 million litres of blood a year and three billion beats in a lifetime.

538. 99% of the calcium contained in the human body is in one's teeth and bones.

539. Human decomposition begins around 4 minutes after death, a process known as 'self-digestion' where your enzymes and bacteria eat you away.

540. As you read this sentence, 50,000 cells in your body died and were replaced by new ones.

541. NFL players are three to four times more likely to contract Alzheimer's disease, Parkinson's disease and Lou Gehrig's disease than an average American. A study found that players in speed positions like wide receivers and running backs were three times more likely to develop neurodegenerative disease than players in non-speed or lineman positions.

542. Heart disease kills more people per year than cancer, war, terrorism, hunger, suicide, diabetes, respiratory diseases and mental disorders combined.

543. Your left lung is about 10 percent smaller than your right one.

544. It always helps to "let it out". Crying decreases the feelings of anger or sadness.

545. Cancers are primarily environmental diseases with 90-95% of cases attributed to environmental factors and 5-10% due to genetics.

546. The liver is perhaps the most resilient of the major organs. It can regenerate from only 25% of its tissue mass. It will even grow to be just the right size for the body it's in.

547. Three to five pounds of your body is made up of bacteria. Between 100 million to 1 billion bacteria can grow on each tooth.

548. There is a disease called anti-NMDA receptor encephalitis, caused when the body's immune system goes haywire and attacks a protein in the brain. Some speculate anti-NMDA receptor encephalitis could be behind historical descriptions of what was believed to be demonic possession.

549. A woman's heartbeat is, on average, faster than a man's by almost eight beats a minute.

550. In terms of compression strength, the femur bone of a person weighing 83kg with size 11 feet could withstand the weight of 16,000 people standing on it at one time.

551. Human teeth are just as strong as shark teeth. They definitely have us beat in sharpness however!

552. Contrary to what they told you in high school, alcohol does not kill brain cells. What excessive alcohol consumption can do is damage the connective tissue at the end of neurons.

553. Synesthesia is a condition that causes senses to overlap which means that some people can hear the sound of colors or taste certain words.

554. The longest beard measures 7 feet 9 inches and belongs to Sarwan Singh of Canada.

555. If all the DNA in your body were uncoiled, it would stretch out to about 10 billion miles, which is the distance from Earth to Pluto and back.

556. Humans are the only species known to blush. When you blush, the lining of your stomach does too!

557. If you had a few too many drinks and can't remember what you did last night, it's not because you forgot. While you are drunk, your brain is incapable of forming memories.

558. More germs are transferred by shaking hands than kissing.

559. The strongest bone in the body is the femur, which is 48cm long and so strong that it can support 30 times the weight of an average man.

560. The first heart cell starts to beat as early as 4 weeks.

561. The average small intestine is about 23 feet long.

562. Human brains have gotten significantly smaller over the past 10-20,000 years. The lost volume is equivalent to the size of a tennis ball.

563. An average male produces more than 500 billion sperm cells in his lifetime.

564. Fingerprints increase friction and help grip objects.

565. The number of heart attacks peaks on Christmas Day.

566. Brain cells cannibalize themselves as a last-ditch source of energy to ward off starvation.

567. The indent under your nose, called the philtrum, is a residual reminder of your time in the womb. In utero, the two sides of your face develop independently, then join at the middle. When the two sides fail to fuse properly, the result is a cleft palate.

568. In a typical group of 50 African monkeys, there are more genetic variations than in the entire human race.

569. If the human eye were a digital camera, it would have 576 megapixels. That's better than any camera on the market! An eye can distinguish about 10 million different colors.

570. Studies show that people with a high IQ dream more often and vividly.

571. The brains of introverts and extroverts are noticeably different. In the brains of extroverts, MRIs reveal that the dopamine reward network is more active. Introverts display more gray matter.

572. There is enough iron in a body to make a metal nail measuring up to three inches long.

573. The first pacemakers for the heart had to be plugged into a wall socket.

574. Over 50% of the dust in your home is actually dead skin.

575. Ninety minutes of sweating can temporarily shrink the brain more than one year of aging does.

576. It IS possible to sneeze with your eyes open, but in most cases your body's response to blink kicks in.

577. When a pregnant woman experiences some kind of an organ damage (a heart attack, for example), the fetus can help with the recovery process as it sends stem cells to the damaged area.

578. It takes up to 6 months for babies to develop their permanent skin tone.

579. You are about 1 centimeter shorter at night. This is because the cartilage between your bones is compressed throughout the day.

580. Lung cancer is the world's most killing cancer. It claims about 1.2 million victims a year. Experts say around 90 percent of lung cancer cases are due to tobacco smoking.

581. Allergies are the result of your immune system reacting to a false alarm. When you experience an allergic reaction, your immune system is responding to a harmless allergen that it perceives as a threat.

582. Humans have more brain cells at the age of two than at any other point in their lives, but it takes nearly 20 years for the brain to mature.

583. A pumping human heart can squirt blood 10 yards.

584. The cracking sound made by knuckles, necks, backs, and other joints is that of bubbles popping in the joints' fluid.

585. Human feet have 500,000 sweat glands and can produce more than a pint of sweat a day!

586. The muscles of the eyes used to focus move around 100,000 times a day. To get the same workout with your leg muscles, you would need to walk 50 miles every day.

587. If the lining of epithial cells which produce mucus were to disappear from your stomach, your stomach would digest itself.

588. Every single person has an individual, unique smell. Identical twins, however, share the same smell.

589. Research has found that emotional content of music and the listener's personal attachment to music can influence pupil dilation.

590. From 1991 to 2000, the average weight of Americans increased by 8.5 pounds.

591. It is not possible to tickle yourself. The brain can predict sensations when your own movement causes them but not when someone else does. Go ahead, try it!

592. Your brain is 73% water. It takes only 2% dehydration to affect your attention, memory and other cognitive skills.

593. The typical human sneeze travels at just under 40 mph. It can almost outrun a tiger!

594. Your olfactory sensory organs shut down during REM sleep. That means that any smell that would normally stimulate a reaction isn't going to do a thing during sleep... including smoke. Now would be a good time to check the batteries in your smoke alarm!

595. Your body produces enough heat in only thirty minutes to boil a half-gallon of water.

596. Like fingerprints, every human tongue has a unique tongue print. Furthermore, every person has a unique set of teeth. Not even identical twins share that similarity!

597. Your appendix is basically useless. While it does produce some white blood cells, most people are fine with an appendectomy.

598. Humans have the most endurance when it comes to long-distance running. Thousands of years ago, we used to run after the prey to hunt until they no longer had energy to continue.

599. Babies in the womb grow 8,000 new brain cells every second. Newborn babies can recognize their mother's face after just a few hours.

600. A foreskin, the size of a postage stamp, from circumcised babies takes only 21 days to grow skin that can cover four football fields. The laboratory-grown skin is used in treating burn patients.

Music

601. An Australian study found that pop and rock stars die 25 years younger than the average person and have higher rates of death by accident and homicide.

602. There is a metal band called *Hatebeak* whose lead singer is an African grey parrot.

603. Krystian Zimerman, an accomplished Polish pianist is known for traveling with his own Steinway grand piano. He was headed to play at Carnegie Hall shortly after 9/11, but his piano was confiscated at JFK Airport by customs officials because the glue smelled "funny". They destroyed the instrument.

604. When German fighter ace Hans-Joachim Marseille was asked to play the piano in front of Hitler, he played a jazz song. This was considered degenerate in Nazi ideology and a demonstration of a lack of respect for the Nazi elite.

605. The tension of the 230-odd strings in a grand piano exert a combined force of 20 tons on the cast iron frame.

606. The most expensive musical instrument in the world is a Stradivarius cello from 1711 that sold for $20 million in 2008.

607. Music in dreams is considered quite rare. According to one study from MIT, about 40 percent of musicians' dreams contain musical content, but in non-musicians that number drops down to about 18 percent.

608. Tim Storms who is known to have the deepest human voice, can hum 8 octaves below the lowest G on the piano. It is so low that humans can't hear it.

609. The London Symphony Orchestra was booked to travel on the Titanic's maiden voyage, but they changed boats at the last minute.

610. A person's heart rate changes while listening to music, but whether the heart beats faster or slower depends on the tempo of the music.

611. Renaissance composer Orlando de Lassus was kidnapped three times as a boy because of his beautiful singing voice.

612. Before Guns N' Roses, Slash once auditioned for the band Poison.

613. The very beginning of country music can be traced to folk songs played by immigrants that settled in the Appalachian Mountains.

614. A 2007 study found that music, especially classical music, helps plants grow faster.

615. In a farewell performance in 1895, Adelina Patti sang *Violetta* while wearing a spectacular white dress studded with 3,700 diamonds worth £200,000 at the time. That is the equivalent of more than £23 million today.

616. The song "One Horse Open Sleigh" was written as a Thanksgiving tune to honor sleigh races happening in Massachusetts. People liked it so much they altered the lyrics to create the popular Christmas song "Jingle Bells".

617. The Eagles started out as the backup band for Linda Ronstadt.

618. Bruce Springsteen's popular and seemingly patriotic, "Born in The U.S.A." is an anti-American anthem about the Vietnam War.

619. Billy Joel failed to graduate with his class in 1967 because he was missing one credit. After returning home from a 3 a.m. performance at a piano bar, he slept right through an early morning English exam. He was playing to help his mother make ends meet.

620. When John Lennon was asked if Ringo Starr was the best drummer in the world he replied "In the world? He's not even the best drummer in The Beatles!"

621. Ringo Starr is a left-handed drummer who plays a right-handed drum kit, leading to his unique drumming style.

622. The Japanese word "karaoke" comes from a phrase meaning "empty orchestra".

623. Today, pickup trucks and country songs go together like peanut butter and jelly! Few understand however, just how important Henry Ford was in the growth of country music. The genre was struggling in the 1920s, but Ford sponsored and promoted the music because he believed it to be of superior moral quality than other music. Many of the early radio programs and performers stayed afloat because of Ford's involvement.

624. Fast music will make you drink faster and louder music in a bar will make you drink more in a shorter period of time.

625. Rick Allen, the drummer for Def Leppard, lost his arm after a car accident in 1984. He thought he could never play in the band again. He learned to play on a customized drum kit that allowed him to trigger the snare drum with the foot normally used for his hi-hat pedals. He returned to the band in 1986.

626. According to the Guinness Book of World Records, Queen has the longest-running fan club.

627. When played live, John Bonham's drum solo on "Moby Dick" would last as little as 6 minutes or, more frequently, as long as 30 minutes, while the rest of the band would leave the stage. At times, it would get so intense that his sticks would break and he'd continue playing with his hands, occasionally drawing blood.

628. During the 1989 US invasion of Panama, the U.S. military blasted AC/DC at General Noriega's compound for two days straight, along with other psychological warfare. The dictator surrendered.

629. Jimi Hendrix created the song "Little Wing" in 145 seconds.

630. Led Zeppelin came up with the title "Black Dog" after a black Labrador walked into the studio during a recording.

631. David Grohl was the only band member of Foo Fighters when recording the first album. He wrote and recorded all vocal, guitar, bass, and drum tracks himself, with the exception of a guest guitar spot.

632. Metallica wrote the song "The God That Failed" because Hetfield's mother died due to Christian beliefs influencing her decision to reject cancer treatment.

633. "Love Is an Open Door" from *Frozen* is the first time a Disney Princess sang a duet with the villain.

634. Merle Haggard did three years at San Quentin for robbery, Steve Earle did time for drugs and Johnny Paycheck served two years for shooting a man. Surprisingly, the man behind "Folsom Prison", Johnny Cash, only spent time in prison when he was performing there.

635. Warner Music Group collects approximately $2 million per year in licensing fees for the song "Happy Birthday to You".

636. Jack White of the White Stripes was saving the "Seven Nation Army" guitar riff in case he got asked to do a James Bond theme. When the band decided that the offer would be unlikely, they decided to incorporate the riff into a song.

637. Lynyrd Skynyrd got their name from a high school teacher, Leonard Skinner, who suspended students for having long hair.

638. The chills you get when you listen to music, is many times caused by the brain releasing dopamine while anticipating the peak moment of a song.

639. Paul McCartney performed at the 2012 London Olympics Opening Ceremony for a fee of only 1 pound.

640. Mary Costa's first paid job as a singer was as the voice of Princess Aurora in *Sleeping Beauty*. It was certainly not her last. She would go on to become an internationally well-known opera singer.

641. A song that gets stuck in your head on repeat is called an earworm.

642. "When You Wish Upon a Star," from *Pinocchio*, was the first Disney song to win the Academy Award for Best Original Song.

643. Kelly Clarkson's "Since U Been Gone" was turned down by P!nk and almost went to Hillary Duff, who didn't have the range for it.

644. It is said that during his career with The Who, Pete Townshend has smashed more than 90 guitars, including at least 23 Fender Stratocasters, 12 Gibson Les Pauls and 21 Gibson SGs.

645. Ironically, Barry Manilow didn't write his song, "I Write the Songs".

646. In 2006, Derek Amato suffered a major concussion from diving into a shallow swimming pool. When he woke up in the hospital, things were very different. He was suddenly very good at piano. He is one of just a few dozen known as "sudden savants" or "accidental geniuses".

647. In 2000, ABBA turned down $1 billion and the opportunity to do a 100-concert reunion tour.

648. Keith Richards came up with the riff for "Satisfaction (I Can't Get No)" in his sleep. He heard the famous three-note riff in his dreams, woke up woke up to record the riff and mumble the words, "I can't get no satisfaction", and fell back to sleep.

649. AC/DC guitarist Malcolm Young worked in a bra factory as a sewing-machine mechanic.

650. Willie Nelson has used the same guitar since 1969. It is a Martin N-20 he calls "Trigger."

651. Sarah McLachlan stated that the inspiration for "Angel" came from learning about how widespread heroin addiction was in the music industry and how fellow musicians were being "picked off by it."

652. Rapper NoClue set the world record in 2005 for fastest rapper by rapping 723 syllables in 51.27 seconds.

653. James Taylor gives free online guitar lessons.

654. According to lyricist Stephen Schwartz, the lyrics to "Colors of the Wind" from *Pocahontas* were inspired by the letter that Chief Seattle wrote to Congress in 1854.

655. Bob Dylan's sunburst Fender Stratocaster, first debuted at the 1965 Newport Folk Festival, sold at auction for a record-breaking $965,000. It is one of the world's most iconic instruments, as it was the night Dylan first "went electric".

656. On his debut album *For You*, released when he was 20, Prince is said to have played all 27 featured instruments.

657. Upon receiving his first guitar, John Lennon's Aunt Mimi told him, "The guitar's all very well, John, but you'll never make a living out of it." A few years later, The Beatles formed.

658. Aerosmith's "I Don't Want to Miss a Thing" was originally written for Celine Dion.

659. American composer John Cage composed a work in 1952 entitled "4' 33", which consists of four minutes and thirty-three seconds of silence.

660. Elvis recorded more than 600 songs, but he didn't write a single one.

661. When Beethoven heard Mauro Giuliani playing the guitar, he said that the instrument was "a miniature orchestra in itself".

662. Peabo Bryson and Regina Belle's rendition of "A Whole New World" is the only Disney song from an animated film to go to Number 1 on the *Billboard* Hot 100.

663. Guns N' Roses' "Sweet Child o' Mine" was written in five minutes.

664. Leo Fender, who developed the first solid-body electric guitar and electric bass guitar, never learned to play either instrument.

665. Jimi Hendrix's tombstone has a Fender Stratocaster carved on it.

666. Metallica is the first and only band to perform on all seven continents after playing a concert in Antarctica called "Freeze 'em All". They hit all continents in a single calendar year.

667. Neil Young's "After the Gold Rush" is the only album reviewed by Rolling Stone Magazine twice. The first time, it was given a poor review. The second time, after the album became such a huge success, it was given an outstanding review.

668. For Christmas 1936, Salvador Dalí sent Harpo Marx a harp with barbed-wire strings. Harpo replied with a photograph of himself with bandaged fingers.

669. Tin Pan Alley in the side streets off of Times Square in New York City received its nickname when, for generations, music publishers auditioned new songs in the 1800s. The awful sound of cheap tinny pianos coming through the open office windows of hundreds of publishers was likened to the beating of tin pans.

670. Dimebag Darrell, former guitarist of metal band Pantera, once asked Eddie van Halen for a copy of his black-and-yellow "Bumblebee" guitar. Eddie agreed, but forgot to follow through. After Dimebag was killed, he showed up at the viewing with the original, which is now buried with him in his "Kiss Kasket".

671. Angelina Jolie's uncle, Chip Taylor, wrote the song "Wild Thing".

672. When John Williams first played the theme song of the film "Jaws" by playing just two notes on a piano, Steven Spielberg is said to have laughed, thinking it was a joke.

673. A bathroom attendant inspired Donna Summer to write the song "She Works Hard for the Money". She went to the bathroom at a Grammy's party and saw the attendant asleep. She told ABC News' *Nightline* that her first thought was, "God, she works hard for her money, that lady". She started writing the song on a piece of toilet paper.

674. How's this for working under pressure? Eminem's "The Real Slim Shady" was written 3 hours before the final cut of the album was due to the record company.

675. A 2015 study revealed that babies remain soothed twice as long when listening to a song than when listening to talking.

676. The longest piano piece of any kind is 'Vexations' by Erik Satie. It consists of a 180-note composition which, on the composer's orders, must be repeated 840 times. Its first reported public performance in September 1963, in the Pocket Theater, New York City, required a relay team of 10 pianists. The performance took 18 hours. The New York Times critic fell asleep at 4 a.m. and the audience dwindled down to 6 people.

677. Barry White served 4 months in jail at the age of 17 for stealing thirty thousand dollars-worth of tires.

678. Canadian astronaut Chris Hadfield released an album of songs entirely recorded in space.

679. The harmonica is the world's best-selling musical instrument.

680. In 1957, Chuck Berry created Berry Park in Missouri, his own interracial amusement park with a guitar shaped swimming pool, in response to the whites-only country clubs from where he was once excluded. Berry died at Berry Park.

681. 1 in 10,000 people have perfect pitch, the ability to recognize a pitch without any reference.

682. Niccolò Paganini, known as the "devil's violinist", was thought by many to be the greatest Violin Virtuoso of all time. He was so talented that many thought he was the Son of the Devil or he had sold his soul for his talent.

683. An advertising company approached Johnny Cash's estate asking for permission to use "Ring of Fire" on an advertisement for hemorrhoid cream. The request was quickly refused.

684. Comedian Jon Benjamin, known for the voice of Archer and Bob from Bob's Burgers, has an entire jazz album where he plays piano, despite not knowing how to actually play the piano. It includes several tracks titled "I Can't Play Piano".

685. One of the first typewriters was originally called a "literary piano."

686. John Mayer became interested in the guitar after watching Michael J. Fox's guitar performance as Marty McFly in the prom scene of "Back to the Future".

687. Since 2012, three major corporate labels have secured control over roughly 90% of the music market. These three corporations are Universal Music Group, Sony Music Entertainment, and Warner Music Group.

688. There is a violin made out of stone called the "Blackbird" that is fully playable.

689. Billy Crystal's father owned a Manhattan record store and produced jazz concerts. Billy's backstage babysitter once was Billie Holiday.

690. BBC reported that cows produce more milk when listening to relaxing music. Cows need stress relief too!

691. The first pressed CD in the United States was Bruce Springsteen's "Born in the USA".

692. Pink Floyd's "Money" has the first curse word that was regularly played on the radio.

693. An intoxicated Eric Clapton once showed up to George Harrison's house, silently handed him a guitar and amp, and the two had a musical duel for 2 hours. Nothing was said, but the general feeling was that Eric won the musical duel.

694. Actor Joe Pesci started as a singer, guitar player and played in the same set as Jimi Hendrix.

695. In 2006, Wallace Hartley's violin was confirmed found in a British man's attic. It was sold at an auction in 2013 for $1.7 million. Hartley is famous for leading the band that played to calm passengers as the Titanic sank on April 15th 1912.

696. Frank Sinatra was buried with a bottle of Jack Daniel's whiskey, a pack of cigarettes, a lighter, and a dollar's worth of dimes, according to news accounts. The dimes were reportedly in case he needed to use a pay phone.

697. Before becoming an actor, Johnny Depp dreamed of becoming a rock star. He has played guitar for Marilyn Manson, Oasis, and Aerosmith.

698. We mishear lyrics because of the powerful role expectations play in our hearing. The meaning we create from songs doesn't come entirely from what we hear.

699. According to research, music can assist in repairing brain damage. Patients with left-side brain damage who can no longer speak find they are able to sing words.

700. Music helps you exercise! It can distract you from physical fatigue.

Travel / The World

701. "Taumatawhakatangihangakoauauotamatea-turipukakapikimaungahoronukupokaiwhenuakitanatahu" is the longest name of a place on Earth. It translates roughly as "The summit where Tamatea, the man with the big knees, the slider, climber of mountains, the land-swallower who travelled about, played his nose flute to his loved one".

702. Switzerland is unique in having enough nuclear fallout shelters to accommodate its entire population, in the event that they are ever needed.

703. France is the most visited country in the world.

704. Blue Lake, in New Zealand's Nelson Lakes National Park, has the clearest water in the world.

705. There is a garbage swirl in the ocean known as the Great Pacific Garbage Patch that is the size of Texas.

706. The city of Chicago is where the first ever Ferris Wheel was invented in the 1893 World's Fair.

707. In Japan, allowing a sumo wrestler make your baby cry is considered to be good for their health.

708. In 1986, Lake Nyos in Africa killed 1,700 villagers and 3,500 livestock overnight when it suddenly released between 100,000 and 300,000 tons of carbon dioxide, suffocating everything within 16 miles. It is still unknown what triggered the event.

709. With more than 3 million lakes, Canada has the most lakes in the world.

710. The Great Smoky Mountain National Park is actually the most visited national park in the United States. They can see more than 11 million visitors a year! It contains more than

800 miles of hiking trails across North Carolina and Tennessee.

711. When three-letter airport codes became standard, airports that had been using two letters simply added an "X".

712. If you keep going North, you will eventually go South. If you keep going East, you will never go West.

713. The German city of Konstanz, which sits on the Swiss border, survived World War 2 without being bombed by leaving all house and streetlights lit at night, making Allied bombers raiding nearby Dornier and Zeppelin aircraft factories think it was part of Switzerland.

714. Honolulu is the only place in the U.S. that has a royal palace.

715. Russia has a larger surface area than Pluto, has a smaller population than the country of Bangladesh.

716. The best-preserved meteor crater in the world is in Winslow, Arizona.

717. There's a bar in South Africa called *Sunland Big Baobab*. It is inside a 6,000-year-old baobab tree, a species which naturally begins to hollow after it reaches about 1,000 years old.

718. Monaco is smaller than Central Park in New York City.

719. More than 25% of Costa Rica is set aside and protected. It has 27 national parks, 58 wildlife refuges, 32 protected zones, 15 wetland areas/mangroves, 11 forest reserves and 8 biological reserves, as well as 12 other conservation regions that protect the distinctive and diverse natural habitats found throughout the country.

720. In Bern, Switzerland, there is a 500-year-old statue of a man eating a sack of babies and nobody is sure why. But *everyone* is sure that it is creepy.

721. Hartsfield-Jackson Airport in Atlanta is the world's busiest airport.

722. Pilots and copilots are required to eat different meals in case one of the meals causes food poising. Usually the pilot gets the first-class meal and the copilot the business class meal.

723. Switzerland has no official capital city.

724. The San Alfonso del Mar resort in Chile has the world's largest swimming pool. It holds 66 million gallons. It also holds the Guinness World Record for being the world's deepest (115 feet). The nearly 20-acre pool sucks water directly in from the sea using a computer-controlled suction and filtration system.

725. Switzerland has more millionaires than recipients of social assistance. Nearly 10% of households in the country have $1 million or more, more than double that of the United States.

726. Las Vegas, Nevada has the most hotel rooms of any city in the world.

727. There is psychology behind casino design. Las Vegas casinos have no clocks or windows so people will lose track of time and spend more money.

728. Colorado is the only state in history, to turn down the Olympics. In 1976 the Winter Olympics were planned to be held in Denver. 62% of all state Voters choose at almost the last minute not to host the Olympics, because of the cost, pollution and population boom it would have on the State of Colorado, and the City of Denver.

729. The "smoke-line" left by an airplane is really water vapor. A longer lasting, wider line could be the sign of an impending storm while a short-lasting line indicates low-humidity air and fair weather.

730. Wood Buffalo National Park in Canada that is larger than Switzerland.

731. The statue of Christ the Redeemer in Rio de Janeiro weighs 635 tons, is 38 meters high and was named one of the "New Seven Wonders of the World" in 2007. It was damaged by a lightning strike in 2014.

732. The highest peak in Europe is in Italy. Monte Bianco is 15,771 feet high and is part of the Alps.

733. The tallest mountain in the world, Mauna Kea, is located in Hawaii. It's about twice the base to peak height of Mount Everest and when measured from the seafloor is over 32,000 feet high. However, Everest is named King because mountains are usually measure from sea level.

734. Ethiopia follows a calendar that is seven years behind the rest of the world.

735. In Singapore, selling, importing or spitting out chewing gum is illegal. Minister Lee Kuan Yew believed gum would trash the country's pavement and subway carts.

736. A British scientist in Botswana started painting eyes on the backside of cows to stop lions from attacking them. He believes that if he can stop African lions killing farmers' cattle, then farmers will stop killing the endangered lions.

737. All the money that is tossed into Rome's Trevi Fountain is collected each night and donated to multiple charities.

738. Africa is the only continent that is in all four hemispheres. (Northern, Southern, Western, Eastern)

739. The world's longest land tunnel is the Lötschberg Base Tunnel, which proves a 22-mile railway link between Switzerland and Italy.

740. The population of Ireland is still approximately 2 million less than it was before the potato famine, 160 years ago.

741. The most expensive hotel room in the world costs $83,200 a night at the Royal Penthouse Suite in Geneva at Hotel President Wilson. It has 12 bedrooms, 12 bathrooms and a wrap-around terrace with impressive views of the Alps.

742. The distance between Europe and Africa is only 36 miles. By ferry, it will take you only half an hour to reach Africa from Spain.

743. Greece has more archaeological museums than any other country in the world.

744. The Leaning Tower of Pisa was built in 1173. By the time builders had finished the third of eight planned stories about five years later, the tower's foundation had begun to settle unevenly on the ground beneath it. Despite various attempts to reinforce it, Pisa's tower continued to tilt at a rate of some 0.05 inches per year, placing it in increasing danger of collapse.

745. In total, the Great Wall of China took more than 2,000 years to build. Construction began in 770 BC and was finally completed in 1633 AD. It is 13,000 miles long!

746. Austrian citizens are said to have the most vacation time of any country. Austria guarantees workers a legal minimum of 22 paid vacation days and 13 paid holidays each year.

747. The most visited amusement park is the Magic Kingdom in Florida. It sees over 20 million people a year.

748. Saudi Arabia does not have a single river.

749. Greece enjoys more than 250 days of sunshine. That's 3,000 sunny hours a year!

750. The Dora Sarchese winery near Ortona, Italy, recently installed a 24-hour wine fountain, which works like a push-button drink fountain. All are welcome to use the fountain for free, except for "drunkens" and "louts".

751. Spain and Portugal provide most of the world's cork. Cork trees flourish in the dry Meseta region in Spain.

752. In one year, China goes through roughly 45 billion pairs of the throwaway utensils; that averages out to nearly 130 million pairs of chopsticks a day. Greenpeace China has estimated that in order to keep up with this demand, 100 acres of trees need to be felled every 24 hours!

753. There are no laws against public nudity in Spain.

754. The Fortingall Yew is an ancient European tree in the churchyard of the village of Fortingall in Perthshire, Scotland. Modern experts estimate its age to be between 2,000 and 3,000 years old. This makes it one of the oldest known trees in Europe, although the root system of the Norway spruce, Old Tjikko, in Sweden is at least 9,500 years old.

755. When traveling to Switzerland there is one rule that you must know before you get there. Using salt and pepper to season your food at a restaurant is considered to be very offensive to the ones preparing the meal. Don't insult your chef by reaching for the seasoning!

756. India produces about 70% of the world's spices.

757. In the 1980's, Robert Crandall, then head of American Airlines, made the deal with airline food, which saved the company $40,000 a year by removing one olive from each in-flight salad.

758. The Eiffel Tower was constructed in 1889 for the World's Fair that year. Originally intended as a temporary exhibit, the Eiffel Tower was almost torn down and scrapped in 1909. It was considered to be something of an eyesore by the Parisians, due to its 1,063-foot height and unusual shape. Now, it is one of the most recognizable structures on the planet and welcomes more visitors than any other paid monument in the world.

759. Around 90 percent of the fresh water on the Earth's surface is held in the ice sheet in Antarctica. That's an amount equivalent to 70 m of water in the world's oceans.

760. The Rio Tinto River in Spain is so polluted by toxic pollution from 5,000 years of mining that it contains little to no life.

761. London has more Indian restaurants than Mumbai or Delhi.

762. In Taiwan, there are prison and hospital-themed restaurants. The most peculiar of them all, however, is a restaurant called "Modern Toilet" that serves food on miniature toilets.

763. The Nasa Vehicle Assembly Building in Florida is so large that it has its own weather. On humid days, rain clouds can form below the ceiling, requiring about 10,000 tons of air conditioning equipment to control the moisture.

764. Sudan has more than 200 pyramids, more than the number of pyramids found in Egypt.

765. Antarctica is the only continent without a native species of ants.

766. Italy is said to have more masterpieces per square mile than any other country in the world.

767. There are up to 200 languages spoken in the city of Manchester, England at any one time. Given its population size of 480,000, that makes it the most linguistically dense and diverse city in Western Europe, if not the world!

768. The ancient Roman Aqueduct of Segovia in Spain was built in the 1st century A.D. and still supplies water to the city.

769. Vatican City is the smallest country in the world. It is governed as an absolute monarchy with the pope at its head. The Vatican mints its own euros, prints its own stamps, issues passports and license plates, operates media outlets and has its own flag and anthem. It even has its own army, the historic Swiss Guard. The only function it lacks is taxation, but museum admission fees, stamp and souvenir sales, and contributions generate the Vatican's revenue.

770. Greece is the world's third leading producer of olives. They have cultivated olive trees since ancient times and some olive trees planted in the thirteenth century are still producing olives!

771. Continuously inhabited for over 7,000 years, Athens is one of the oldest cities in Europe.

772. The Parthenon was built almost 2,500 years ago and sits on the Acropolis above the city of Athens. It took 8 or 9 years to build and, while only ruins remain today, featured a massive ivory-and-gold statue of Athena.

773. Minnesota is the unofficial Norwegian capital of the United States, and more Norwegians live in Minnesota than in any other state.

774. Only 1% of the items kept at the British Museum are actually on display.

775. Even though Norway is one the biggest exporters of oil in the world, Norway has the highest gasoline prices in the world at $9.79 dollars per gallon.

776. The last meal on Noah's ark, a sweet and sour pudding called aşure, is still served as a dessert throughout Turkey. It is said to have contained 40 different ingredients, which were the remainders of his supplies.

777. Strip clubs have been banned from Iceland since 2010. It was banned for feminist reasons, rather than religious.

778. The airport in Brussels sells more chocolate than any other location on Earth.

779. There are ZERO mosquitoes in Iceland! There is no definite explanation as to why the country remains mosquito-free.

780. Angel Falls in Venezuela is the highest waterfall in the world at almost 1000 meters high

781. In winter, the icicles hanging from the gutters in Moscow are so enormous, weighing hundreds of pounds, that they could kill or severely injure those below. An elite group of amateur mountaineers, who use ropes and climbing equipment to get to drainpipes and overhanging eaves.

782. Traffic in Moscow is so bad that wealthy Russians hire fake ambulances to beat the jams.

783. Russia has 11 time zones. More than any other country.

784. Every year, thousands of snakes gather at the Narcisse Snake Dens in Manitoba, Canada. It is the largest gathering of snakes anywhere in the world.

785. Canada is home to 15,500 of the world's 25,000 polar bears.

786. Because of its sheer length, the Himalayan mountain system stretches across six countries: Afghanistan, Bhutan, India, Nepal, Pakistan and Tibet.

787. Every 1 person out of 10 successful climbers reach the peak of the Mount Everest but die there.

788. Reinhold Messner was the first to climb Everest all alone and with no oxygen. He achieved this great accomplishment in 1980.

789. It took 22,000 workmen and 22 years to complete The Taj Mahal.

790. The Sagrada Familia church in Barcelona is taking longer to build than the pyramids. Iit was started in 1882 and it is still under construnction.

791. Vietnam is also home to the world's largest cave, Son Doong.

792. In China, it is not uncommon to come across canned fresh air for sale due to the rampant air pollution that has rocked the country. One company, Green & Clean Air, sells $20 bottles holding about 130 breaths from various locations in Australia.

793. Wild orangutans are found in only two places on earth: Sumatra in Indonesia and the island of Borneo. Orangutans are one of the biggest victims of habitat loss due to poor palm oil practices.

794. Istanbul's Kapalıçarşı, or Grand Bazaar, is among the world's largest covered markets. It is spread across 64 streets, with around 4,000 shops, and 25,000 workers. It is also among the oldest markets, dating back to 1520. The market gets approximately 400,000 visitors a day!

795. The oldest known human city is Çatalhöyük in Turkey, which shows signs of settlement from the 7th century B.C.

796. Istanbul is the world's only city spanning two continents. Three percent is in Europe and 97% in Asia.

797. Turkey has 82,693 mosques, more than any other country per capita in the world. Researchers say the number of mosques has grown from 60,000 in 1987 to more than 85,000 in 2015.

798. Founded in 1752 as an imperial menagerie by Emperor Franz Stephan, Vienna's Schönbrunn Tiergarten is the oldest zoo in the Western World.

799. The magic words for wine drinkers in Vienna are *ein Achtel*, which translates to an eighth of a liter. It is the most common serving size in Vienna.

800. Rest, relaxation, and ... radioactivity? Due to the fact that the waters at the Austrian spa Bad Gastein contain radon, patients must produce a doctor's order before enjoying the spa's healing waters.

Art

801. There is a second "Mona Lisa" painting held in a secret vault in Switzerland also thought to have been painted by Leonardo da Vinci that shows a much younger version of the female subject. It has been the subject of much debate and analysis, as it was painted on canvas, while Leonardo painted mostly on wood.

802. Vincent Van Gogh produced more than 2,000 works during his life: 900 paintings and 1,100 drawings and sketches, but struggled to make a living as an artist. He only sold one painting, *The Red Vineyard*, while he was alive.

803. In 1955, someone dropped a 600-year-old plaster Buddha statue that was being relocated. When the installers inspected the damage, they discovered the plaster was actually covering a solid gold statue. Its estimated monetary value alone is close to $250 million.

804. An anonymous French urban artist, Invader, has spent the last twenty years installing over 3300 Space Invaders mosaics in 60 cities all around the world.

805. In 2011, a woman named Aimee Davison purchased a "non-visible" piece of art titled "Fresh Air" for $10,000.

806. St Sebastian, a Christian saint, is often depicted in art during his death, with arrows impaling his body. An artist named Michael Richards has a piece where he cast a mold of himself and, instead of arrows, had planes flying into his body. Richards died on the 92nd floor of the North Tower on 9/11.

807. Georges Braque was the first living person to have art displayed in Louvre.

808. Two con men sold a forged Goya painting, only to find out that the 1.7 million Swiss Francs were counterfeit when they attempted to deposit it to a bank in Geneva. They were then detained by French customs, who discovered the fake Swiss Francs in their suitcase, and informed the Spanish authorities.

809. After Leonardo da Vinci's death, King Francis I of France hung the *Mona Lisa* in his bathroom.

810. On December 3rd, 1961, Henri Matisse's painting "Le Bateau" was put right-side up after hanging upside-down for 46 days without anyone noticing at the Museum of Modern Art in New York.

811. A Polish art student hung his own painting up at the National Museum in Poland where it went unnoticed for three days.

812. Leonard da Vinci's *The Last Supper*, which can be seen in the Convent of Santa Maria delle Grazie in Milan, Italy, originally included Jesus' feet. But in 1652, while installing a doorway in the refectory where the painting is on view, builders cut into the bottom-center of the mural, lopping off Jesus' feet.

813. In his early 30s, a drunken Lennon used a valuable painting by French artist Matisse as an ashtray on a visit to the Playboy Mansion in Los Angeles in the Seventies.

814. A man was arrested in Ireland after punching a hole into a 10 million dollar Monet painting. He claimed that his fist fell onto it because he had a heart condition. The artwork was finally restored this year following a painstaking 18-month restoration.

815. Salvador Dali believed he was his dead brother's reincarnation. There is also a portrait or a silhouette of Dali in every one of his paintings. He produced over 1500 paintings, many of them regarded as masterpieces, and nearly single handily kept the mainstream surrealist movement alive.

816. A lost masterpiece by Da Vinci, titled *The Battle of Anghiari* is likely hidden behind a wall in Florence, but nobody is willing to take the wall down because the wall itself has a priceless fresco painted on it.

817. It took Seurat more than two years to complete *A Sunday on La Grande Jatte —1884*, which is made up of millions of dots.

818. On April 15, 1958, *A Sunday on La Grande Jatte —1884 was* on loan at the Museum of Modern Art in New York City when a fire broke out in the adjoining Whitney Museum. The fire damaged six canvases, injured 31 people, and killed one workman, but Seurat's beloved work taken to safety through an elevator evacuation plan.

819. The small town depicted in Vincent van Gogh's *The Starry Night* is Saint-Rémy-de-Provence in the south of France. Van Gogh painted the work while he was a patient at the Saint-Paul-de-Mausole, a psychiatric hospital in Saint-Rémy, so it depicts the view from the east-facing window of his asylum room.

820. The marble slab that would become the sculpture of David by Michelangelo in 1504 was cut 43 years earlier for an artist named Agostino di Duccio, who planned to turn it into a statue of Hercules. Di Duccio abandoned his sculpture and the marble was unused for 10 years until another sculptor, Antonio Rossellino, decided to work with it. Rossellino also abandoned his work because he found marble too difficult to work with. Michelangelo began work on his sculpture in 1501.

821. In 1945, President Roosevelt collapsed while being painted. He suffered a cerebral hemorrhage and died the following day. The unfinished painting captures his last waking moment.

822. Edgar Degas was so fascinated with ballet dancers that he became obsessed with representing them in his art. It is estimated Degas made approximately 1500 paintings, pastels, prints and drawings of dancers.

823. Pablo Picasso's first word was the Spanish word for pencil.

824. Van Gogh created *Portrait of Dr. Gachet* in appreciation for the doctor that opened up his home to Van Gogh after coming out of the asylum.

825. There are technically five separate versions of Expressionist artist Edvard Munch's most famous work, *The Scream*. One version, done in 1910 by Munch due to the popularity of the previous incarnations, made headlines in 1994 for being stolen from a Norwegian art museum. Two thieves broke through a window of the National Gallery, cut a wire holding the painting to the wall and left a note reading "Thousand thanks for the bad security!" It was recovered 3 months later in a daring undercover operation by British detectives.

826. Picasso's abstract depiction of five Barcelona prostitutes was deemed immoral when it debuted at the artist's studio in 1907.

827. Andy Warhol was a hoarder who would fill warehouses with random items such as mummified feet from Ancient Egypt and Clark Gable's boots.

828. Cai-Guo Qiang is a Chinese contemporary "explosive artist" best known for the opening of the Beijing Olympics in 2008. He creates ethereal artworks traced in flames and gunpowder, using pyrotechnics as a means to communicate with extraterrestrials.

829. An art collector of the Indian-born British sculptor, Anish Kapoor, was awarded £350,000 in damages after an art storage company mistook one piece of work for garbage and threw it away.

830. Andy Warhol's 1962 Pop Art depiction of a Campbell's Soup can is a set of 32 silkscreened canvases, each representing the 32 separate soup varieties that the company sold at the time. Warhol never gave instructions on how to display them, so the Museum of Modern Art arranged them chronologically in the order in which the soups were introduced by the Campbell's.

831. Monet's father disapproved of his painting. He wanted him to go into the family's grocery business.

832. Jean-Michel Basquiat liked to wear Armani suits as he painted and then wear them out later on, still covered in paint.

833. It is believed that *Whistler's Mother* was envisioned to be a portrait of a model. James asked his mother, Anna Whistler, to pose in replacement of a model who did not show up. He had initially envisioned painting the model standing, but his mother found it uncomfortable to stand for a long period of time.

834. *Mona Lisa* has an exclusive room that costs the museum over $6.2 million dollars in renovation costs. It is protected in a climate controlled environment and encased in bullet proof glass.

835. Isabella Stewart Gardner Museum in Boston has not removed empty frames of stolen paintings from the walls after an art theft in 1990. The art stolen is worth at least 500 million and includes the loss of three Rembrandts, a Vermeer, a Manet and sketches by Degas.

836. Norman Rockwell tried to enlist in the military during World War I, but was initially rejected for being 17 pounds underweight at 6 feet tall and only 140 pounds.

837. During the Renaissance, being an artist was not considered a suitable occupation for a gentleman. Since art involved working with hands, artists were considered craftsmen and were given the same social standing as tailors or shoemakers.

838. A British artist named Tim Knowles attaches pens to trees and lets the wind do the rest of the work.

839. Despite his wealth, Michelangelo left something to be desired in the hygiene department. It is said that he never bathed and rarely changed his clothes. In fact, on his deathbed, it is believed that his clothing had to be peeled off of him.

840. On April 6th, 1990, *The Night Watch* became a target of vandalism for the second time, when a man sprayed acid onto the canvas. Security intervened and quickly sprayed water on the canvas. Since the acid had penetrated only the varnish layer of the painting, it was thankfully restored.

841. Georgia O'Keeffe painted in her car to shield herself from the harsh sun present in the desert landscapes she painted.

842. In Van Gogh's *Café Terrace at Night*, artificial gas lanterns lighten the night sky with a glimpse of exterior of a Parisian cafe. The cafe is still there and has been a famous destination for all Van Gogh fans. This is the first painting by Gogh with starry backgrounds.

843. To keep Anish Kapoor's *Cloud Gate* clean, the sculpture is wiped down with a microfiber cloth twice a day with a solution of water and liquid tide. At 33 feet high, 42 feet wide and 66 feet long, labor and maintenance costs for *Cloud Gate* cost around $35,000 annually.

844. Micro-sculptor Willard Wigan creates artwork so small that he once inhaled one by accident. His sculptures sit within the eye of a needle, or pinhead and will cost you about $40,000.

845. Yves Klein was unsatisfied with all of the options available when it came to the color blue, so he created and patented his own.

846. Leonardo Da Vinci was left handed and his personal notes were written in mirror writing starting from the right side of the page to the left.

847. There are only 15 authenticated Leonardo da Vinci in the world. The small number of surviving paintings is due in part to his chronic procrastination, but he also had an artistic philosophy in which he would destroy any art he felt was not perfect.

848. In 2007, Giovanni Maria Pala, an Italian computer technician and musician, stated that he had uncovered musical notes in Da Vinci's famous painting *The Last Supper*. Da Vinci was known to be a music enthusiast who incorporated musical riddles in his writings which must be read from right to left.

849. The subject in the Johannes Vermeer's painting *Girl with The Pearl* Earring is unknown. Researchers strongly suspect that the girl was his daughter, Maria.

850. Aelita Andre is an Australian artist who recently sold $30,000 worth of paintings at a New York exhibition at the age of four. She began to paint when aged nine months, and her work was displayed publicly in a group exhibition shortly after she turned two.

851. Piet Mondrian often worked on paintings until his hands were blistered and he was in tears of frustration. It's impossible to deny Mondrian's influence on the world of art, but it is difficult to understand why straight lines and grids frustrated him so easily.

852. Pablo Picasso was considered a suspect in the theft of Mona Lisa in 1911. He was arrested and questioned, but later cleared and released.

853. Jackson Pollock often used cigarettes to paint.

854. "The Goldfinch" is one of the many masterpieces created by Rembrandt's student, Carel Fabritius. Fabritius died 1654 when a magazine containing at least 90,000 pounds of gunpowder blew up in the heart of Delft. In the explosion, a quarter of the city, including his studio and many of his paintings were destroyed. Only a dozen of his paintings, including "The Goldfinch", survived.

855. A researcher found that 39% of Bob Ross' paintings contain an "almighty mountain", 44% contain at least one "happy cloud", and 18% feature a "charming little cabin".

856. Congo, a chimpanzee who made over 400 paintings, would scream if a painting was taken away from him before he was finished. Pablo Picasso was reportedly a "fan" of his paintings, and hung one of the ape's pictures on his studio wall after receiving it as a gift.

857. Much of Ancient Egyptian art was not meant to be seen by "normal people". The art was created in secret to be viewed by the elite and it was "too powerful to be viewed by the general public".

858. The Renaissance Masterpiece *The Pieta* is the only work that Michelangelo Buonarroti ever signed. He later regretted what he considered an outburst of pride and vowed to never sign another work again

859. Auguste Rodin's work, *The Age of Bronze*, was so realistic people though he sacrificed a real person inside the cast.

860. Modern research shows that the statue of David is not perfect. It turns out that he is crossed – eyed. The scientific community agreed that Michelangelo did this on purpose so that the profile of David would be perfect from different sides.

861. Graffiti artist David Choe who painted the inside of Facebook's first offices chose to be paid in Facebook stock rather than cash which is now worth over 200 million.

862. In 1996, artist Peter von Tiesenhausen claimed legal copyright over his land as a work of art, forcing pipeline developers to do expensive rerouting around it. He charges land developers $500 an hour to meet with him.

863. In 2012, the Smithsonian officially recognized video games as an art form and had an exhibit to "comprehensively examine the evolution of video games as an artistic medium."

864. Mona Lisa was painted with eyebrows and eyelashes, but they have gradually eroded over time, possibly the result of over-cleaning.

865. In 2006, Banksy painted an image of a naked man clinging to the windowsill on a wall of a public family planning clinic. 97% of residents declared they liked the piece and were in favor of it remaining in public view.

866. Until recently, it was assumed that ancient Greek and Rome statues were made from white marble and were of natural colors. However, recent technologies confirmed that they were painted with a palette that displayed a sophisticated understanding of color and shading.

867. An art work made from excess fat from Italian Prime Minister Silvio Berlusconi was sold for $18,000. Switzerland-based artist Gianni Motti claims to have bought the fat from a clinic where the leader had a liposuction operation performed. He molded it into a bar of soap which he named *Clean Hands*.

868. When asked to name his favorite among all his paintings, Pablo Picasso replied "the next one."

869. According to Munch, *The Scream* was inspired the day he was walking with his friends and saw that "the sky turned as red as blood," before feeling incredibly tired and hearing an "enormous infinite scream of nature." While the scream he heard was imagined, the sky was red as a result of the 1883 eruption of Krakatoa in Indonesia. The volcano's impact was felt as far as New York where the sky was reported to be "crimsoned."

870. After the Taliban destroyed the two ancient monumental Buddha statues in 2001, archaeologists discovered a series of ancient caves with 1000-year-old paintings depicting various scenes from Buddhist mythology. They are believed to be the oldest oil paintings ever found.

871. Gustav Klimt, who created the iconic piece *The Kiss*, used cat urine as a fixative. His obsession with cats led him to cover the pages of his sketchbooks with cat urine. He believed it was the best fixative available. The odor was terrible, but worse, he destroyed works that would likely be worth millions today.

872. Sandy Skoglund, an American installation artist and photographer, stages elaborate tableaux. In *Body Limits*, she wrapped a room and everything in it entirely in uncooked bacon.

873. Leonardo da Vinci was an avid vegetarian and would buy caged birds just to let them go.

874. *The Last Supper* has a permanent home is a convent in Milan, Italy. Da Vinci painted the religious work directly on the dining hall wall of the Convent of Santa Maria delle Grazie back in 1495.

875. An American graphic designer named Scott Wade has become famous for his amazing drawings, created using the dirt found on car windows.

876. Cultural success was considered a wartime victory, and the CIA is said to have promoted the abstract expressionist work of artists like Jackson Pollock internationally to make

America appear more progressive and culturally relevant than the Soviet Union.

877. Michelangelo first rose to prominence after a failed attempt at art fraud. He carved a sham cupid that was sold to Cardinal Raffaele Riario under the guise of being a recently recovered archeological wonder. When Riario learned of the scam, he invited Michelangelo to Rome for a meeting.

878. The Statue of Liberty was originally a copper color, but turned green over time due to oxidation.

879. The Washington Monument has graffiti at its base. The monument was still under construction when the Civil War broke out. Union soldiers were posted there and carved their names onto the monument.

880. Learning art correlates strongly with your achievements in math and reading.

881. Norman Rockwell definitely had a type. All three of his wives were schoolteachers.

882. When Pop Art was originally unleashed unto the London masses, it was referred to as Propaganda Art.

883. Before Michelangelo started on the ceiling of the Sistine Chapel in 1508, it had been decorated as a blue night sky with golden stars, painted by the Umbrian artist Piero Matteo d'Amelia.

884. Although many believe Michelangelo painted the ceiling lying on his back, he actually constructed his own scaffolding, so that he could paint standing up for more precision and control.

885. The oldest North American art is said to date back 11,000 BC. In Florida, there was a bone discovered which had a mammoth carved into it.

886. In 2007, Banksy had a live elephant, that he painted pink in his "Barely Legal" exhibition in Los Angeles.

887. Joan Miró befriended a variety of influential writers during his time in Paris. Among them was Ernest Hemingway, who had to win the right to purchase Miró's piece by rolling dice with one of his friends.

888. Picasso mentored Joan Miró in Paris and they went on to become life-long friends.

889. Synesthesia is the cognitive ability to perceive sounds, colors, and/or words through two or more senses simultaneously. A condition that supposedly led Wassily Kandinsky to paint his vibrant, symphonic abstractions.

890. Matisse studied and trained to become a lawyer. He graduated from law school in Paris and worked as a clerk in a law office in 1889.

891. Matisse was in a wheel chair during his later years, which resulted in some of his most well-known cut-out pieces. After he could no longer stand for long periods of time, Matisse began creating works using a pair of scissors and paper. He used a long stick to assemble them on his walls. He called this technique 'painting with scissors'.

892. Grant Wood painted one of the most recognizable works of a farmer and his daughter standing in front of an old farmhouse titled, *American Gothic*. Wood's sister, Nan and his 62-year-old dentist were the models for this painting.

893. René Magritte made money by reproducing paintings by Picasso, Chirico, and Braques. He also printed counterfeit banknotes to help him survive the postwar period.

894. Pieter Bruegel's painting "The Triumph of Death" reveals the devastation of the Black Death. It is said to be one of the most horrifying paintings of the age.

895. Salvador Dali and Walt Disney collaborate on an animated film called Destino. The film's production started back in the mid-1940s, but it was interrupted by the financial realities of life in wartime. Walt Disney Studios did not complete the 10-minute film until 2003.

896. Tim Burton has been a compulsive drawer from an early age. The characters Edward Scissorhands and Jack Skellington both come from his childhood illustrations.

897. Tim Burton studied at the California Institute of Art, then found himself at Disney after graduation. Burton's gothic style is *very* different from the Disney brand. It's no surprise that Burton found himself out-of-place in his short career there.

898. Salvador Dali claims to have gotten the inspiration for the iconic melting clocks in his piece *The Persistence of Memory* from chunks of Camembert cheese he observed melting in the sun. No one is sure if he was joking.

899. The first documented art heist occurred in 1473, when a triptych by the Dutch painter named Hans Memling was stolen from a ship traveling to Florence by Polish pirates. The pirates brought the altarpiece to a cathedral in Gdańsk, Poland, and to this day it remains in Gdańsk's national museum.

900. Three paintings by Van Gogh, Picasso and Gauguin, worth an estimated $8 million, spent an evening in a public bathroom after vanishing from the nearby Whitworth Art Gallery in Manchester. The paintings were found stuffed in a cardboard tube which included a note claiming that the thieves had engineered the heist to highlight poor security at the museum.

Cinema

901. Sean Connery turned down the Gandalf role in *Lord of the Rings* saying, "I read the book. I read the script. I saw the movie. I still don't understand it."

902. Alfred Hitchcock chose not to conclude the film, *The Birds*, with his usual "THE END" title because he wanted to leave the audience with the feeling of unending terror.

903. Surprisingly, the only physical damage made during the filming of *National Lampoon's Animal House* was when John Belushi created a hole in the wall with a guitar. The actual Sigma Nu fraternity house, which was used to portray the Delta House, never repaired it. They framed the hole in honor of the film.

904. Although not as successful as the sequels, the first *"Paranormal Activity"* movie cost less than $15,000 to make, but grossed over $193,000,000.

905. The *Back to the Future* script was rejected 40 times before Universal bought it. Disney turned down the opportunity saying it was a "movie about incest". This is in reference to the 1955 scene in which Marty kisses the 18-year-old version of his mother.

906. The final speech by Gregory Peck in *To Kill a Mockingbird* was done in one take.

907. There is a Starbucks cup in every single scene in the movie *"Fight Club"*. It contributed to the point of the effects that consumerism has on our lives.

908. The locusts in the 1999 film, *The Mummy*, were mostly computer-generated, but some live grasshoppers were used. Hours before filming they were chilled in a refrigerator to make them more sluggish.

909. The first American film to show a flushing toilet on screen was *Psycho*.

910. *300* is the most death-packed film ever made with an average of 5 people dying every minute.

911. Paul Schrader claims he wrote the script for *Taxi Driver* in under a fortnight, as self-therapy, to "exorcise the evil I felt within me".

912. The Disney character Aladdin was modeled after Tom Cruise.

913. The average shot length in the film *Vertigo* is 6.7 seconds.

914. The iconic roar that *Godzilla* makes in the 1954 movie was created by rubbing a leather glove coated in pine-tar resin across the strings of a double bass instrument.

915. The word "dude" in The Big Lebowski is used approximately 161 times in the movie. The "F-word" or a variation of the "F-word" is used 292 times.

916. Voice actors Wayne Anthony Allwine and Russi Taylor, who gave voice to the characters of Mickey and Minnie Mouse, were married in real life!

917. The sound of the velociraptors communicating with each other in *Jurassic Park* is actually the sound of tortoises mating.

918. When you hear the sound of the crowd chanting, "Spartacus! Spartacus!" in the movie Spartacus, it was actually a pre-taped recording from a 1959 football game at Michigan State University's Spartan Stadium.

919. Bollywood is the largest film industry in the world. It produces over 800 movies a year, which is almost twice as many as Hollywood!

920. There are 26 minutes of just staring during the *Twilight* movies.

921. In 1994, during one famous lunch at Pixar after putting the finishing touches on *Toy Story*, director John Lasseter and writers Pete Docter and Joe Ranft brainstormed ideas that would eventually become *A Bug's Life*, *Finding Nemo*, *Monster Inc.* and *Wall-E*. All on the napkins from their table.

922. "101 Dalmatians" and "Peter Pan" are the only two Disney animated movies in which both parents are present and don't die in the movie plot.

923. *Psycho* was released in black and white because Hitchcock was told by many that the shower scene was too gory.

924. The cake in the movie Sixteen Candles is made of cardboard.

925. In *"Charlie & the Chocolate Factory"*, Tim Burton had 40 squirrels trained to crack nuts rather than rely on CGI. The animals were trained every day for 10 weeks before filming commenced.

926. The DeLorean time machine in *Back to the Future* is actually a licensed, registered vehicle in the state of California.

927. The scene in *Pulp Fiction* where Vincent stabs Mia in the heart with a needle was actually shot in reverse. In actuality, John Travolta was pulling the needle out of her.

928. Dan Akroyd's original script for *Ghostbusters* was called "Ghost Smashers" and was set in a future where Ghostbusters were everyday figures of society like policemen and firemen.

929. The famous shot featured in the Bond films' introduction was filmed through the barrel of a gun.

930. The diner in the movie *The Sting* is the same diner interior used in *Back to the Future*.

931. The film *A Beautiful Mind* was shot in sequence in order to help Russell Crowe better develop his character's emotional arc.

932. In the Stephen King novella for *The Shawshank Redemption*, Morgan Freeman's character, Red, is described as a white Irishman. Red's line, "Maybe it's cause I'm Irish" was a sarcastic nod to the change.

933. The title of the movie *Do the Right Thing* comes from a Malcolm X quote: "You've got to do the right thing."

934. The "burning of Atlanta" scene in *Gone with the Wind* was created by setting fire to old sets found on the MGM lot. The burned sets included *King Kong* (1933), *The Last of the Mohicans* (1936), and *Little Lord Fauntleroy* (1936).

935. Only 12 years separates the father and son duo Sean Connery and Harrison Ford in the Indiana Jones franchise.

936. When the star of *Dracula*, Bela Lugosi, died in 1956, he was buried wearing a black silk cape similar to the one he wore in the film.

937. While filming *Poltergeist*, Robbie truly got choked during a take by the robot clown doll. It wasn't until the boy turned purple that Spielberg realized what was actually happening.

938. In *Django Unchained*, there's a scene where Leo DiCaprio smashes a glass in a fit of rage, causing his hand to bleed profusely. This was an accident, but Tarantino kept it in the movie.

939. Vans, the company behind the checkerboard shoes worn by Sean Penn in the cult movie, *Fast Times at Ridgemont High*, became a national brand after the film's release in 1982.

940. Director John McTiernan asked Rickman to fall 25 feet backwards onto an airbag on the count of three. The stunt crew decided to drop him on "one" instead of "three", to make his reaction more genuinely believable.

941. *Silent Hill*'s location is based on a real place in Centralia, Pennsylvania. It's mostly abandoned, but anyone who's ever visited confirms it's really unsettling.

942. The largest number of fatalities ever in a production of a film occurred during the shooting of the 1931 film *Viking*. Twenty-seven people died, including the director and cinematographer, when a ship they were shooting from exploded in the ice off the coast of Newfoundland.

943. Neither Michelle Rodriguez nor Jordana Brewster had drivers' licenses before production of the film in *Fast and the Furious*. Michelle Rodriguez said she has a horrible driving record due to speeding tickets, which isn't surprising knowing where she learned to drive!

944. James Caan originally heard the phrase "bada-bing!" from his acquaintance, the real-life mobster Carmine Persico, and improvised its use in the film *The Godfather*.

945. In 2009, Daniel Radcliffe's stunt double was paralyzed in *Harry Potter and the Deathly Hallows: Part 1*. They worked alongside each other for six movies and became close friends, so Daniel created a fundraiser to pay for his college education.

946. Production for *No Country for Old Men* was interrupted for a day due to a smoke cloud from the set of *There Will Be Blood*, which was also filming in the area.

947. Ed Helms is actually missing a tooth. He got a permanent implant when he was a teenager, so his dentist removed it during filming for *The Hangover*.

948. In *The Wizard of Oz*, the Wicked Witch of the West was severely burned by a flame in the scene where she is leaving Munchkinland after confronting Dorothy.

949. The sirens heard in the casino scene in *Swingers* were police on their way to stop the film makers. They were shooting without a permit.

950. When Alex was being dunked repeatedly in *A Clockwork Orange*, there was an air tube underwater for actor Malcolm McDowell to breathe through. Unfortunately, it got clogged. All of his struggles in scene were real.

951. In the movie *Field of Dreams*, both Ben Affleck and Matt Damon are among the thousands of extras in the Fenway Park scene. Over a decade later, when Phil Alden Robinson worked with Affleck on the production of *The Sum of All Fears*, Affleck said, "Nice working with you again."

952. During the chest-buster scene in *Alien*, the actors were not told that the xenomorph was going to explode from Kane's chest, so their absolutely horrified reactions are real. It even caused Veronica Cartwright to pass out.

953. Dooley Wilson who played Sam in *Casablanca*, was a professional drummer who couldn't play the piano. He simply mimed along, copying a pianist off screen.

954. Tony Todd put actual bees in his mouth while filming this scary *Candyman* scene. He wore a mouth guard to protect himself and to keep the bees from going down his throat, but was stung elsewhere 23 times.

955. The lights over the "facehugger" eggs in *Alien* were provided by Roger Daltrey and The Who. The band were in a villa next to Shepperton Studios experimenting with laser beams for their tour and let Ridley Scott borrow their gear.

956. The voice of Boo from *Monsters, Inc.*, Mary Gibbs, was just a toddler during production. The crew couldn't get her to sit still and read her lines, so they followed her around with a mic while she played in the studio.

957. For the infamous scene in *A Christmas Story* in which Flick's tongue sticks to the frozen flagpole, a hidden suction tube was used to safely create the illusion that his tongue had frozen to the metal.

958. The charcoal drawing of a naked Kate Winslet in *Titanic* was drawn James Cameron.

959. *ET* and *Poltergeist* were originally supposed to be the same movie, called *Night Skies*. *Night Skies* was about a rural family terrorized by an alien invasion. Eventually, that evolved into the more benign arrival of *E.T.*, while the invasive, ghostly force gave us *Poltergeist*.

960. Will Ferrell's reactions during the jack-in-the-box scene in *Elf* were genuine. The director surprised him every time he played with one of the toys by using a remote control.

961. For *Dr. Strangelove*, Peter Sellers was paid $1 million, 55 percent of the film's budget.

962. Jim Caviezel was struck by lightning twice while making the film, *Passion of the Christ*. Once was while filming the Sermon on the Mount scene and a second time reenacting the crucifixion.

963. Michael Caine was so terrified of Heath Ledger's Joker in *The Dark Knight* that he forgot every one of his lines in the first rehearsal they had together.

964. Love actually IS in the airport! The airport greeting footage at the beginning and end of *Love Actually* is real.

Richard Curtis had a team of cameramen film at Heathrow airport for a week, and whenever they saw something that would fit in they asked the people involved for permission to use the footage.

965. The real Frank Abagnale Jr. appears in *Catch Me If You Can* as the French policeman who arrests Leonardo di Caprio.

966. In *The Princess Diaries*, Mia wasn't supposed to trip and fall on the bleachers. That was just a clumsy moment by Anne Hathaway, but director Garry Marshall decided to keep it in the film.

967. In the film *The Invisible Man*, Claude Rains was dressed in black velvet and filmed against a black velvet background to create the effect that he wasn't there.

968. While filming *Home Alone*, Joe Pesci deliberately avoided Macaulay Culkin on set. He wanted Culkin to think he was mean.

969. Actors Patrick Stewart and Ian McKellan had never played a game of chess in their lives until the movie *X-Men* required them to do so.

970. The three main actors in *Rebel Without a Cause*, filmed in 1955, all met a tragic death. James Dean died in a car crash, Natalie Wood drowned, and Sal Mineo was stabbed to death.

971. Paul Bateson, who played a radiologist's assistant in *The Exorcist*, was a convicted murderer who killed gay men in the late '70s.

972. In the first "Spider-Man" movie in 2002, a Steatoda spider was used. It was given anesthesia and then painted blue and red for the scene.

973. For his scene in *Ferris Bueller's Day Off* Charlie Sheen stayed awake for 48-hours to give the desired 'wasted' look.

974. Due to a miscommunication on set in *The Hateful Eight*, Kurt Russell accidentally smashed an antique guitar from 1870 that was on loan from the Martin Guitar Museum thinking it was a prop. You can see Jennifer Jason Leigh scream and look at the crew afterwards. Not surprisingly, the Martin Guitar Museum announced it is no longer loaning to movies.

975. In the 1985 horror film *Day of the Dead*, zombies are actually feasting on turkey legs that were barbecued in a special way to look like human flesh.

976. In *Jurassic Park*, a guitar string was used to make the water ripple on the dash board of the Ford Explorer by attaching it to the underside of the dash beneath the glass.

977. Jim Cameron had a second ending for *Titanic* in which Bill Paxton and the old lady face off over the million-dollar necklace.

978. In *The Exorcist*, Regan, played by Linda Blair, turns her head almost completely around to face backward. To achieve this effect, a dummy with a swivel neck performed the famous scene. The sound of her neck turning was made by twisting an old leather wallet around a microphone.

979. The scene in *Pretty Woman* when Richard Gere snapped the necklace case on Julia Roberts's fingers was a prank, so her reaction was totally natural. It was originally intended to go into the gag reel.

980. Sylvester Stallone wanted to make sure the boxing scenes looked real in *Rocky IV*, so he instructed Dolph Lundgren to actually hit him. A punch to the chest left Stallone in intensive care at St. John's hospital for five days.

981. In Alfred Hitchcock's *The Birds*, live birds were tied to Tippi Hedren while she laid on the floor. She endured five days of filming where handlers hurled ravens, doves and a few pigeons at her while filming the iconic attic scene. Cary Grant told her, "You're the bravest woman I've ever seen".

982. Steven Spielberg nicknamed the mechanical shark in the movie Jaws, "Bruce."

983. Steven Spielberg refused to take payment for *Schindler's List*, considering it "blood money". He wanted all profits to be returned to the Jewish community.

984. Matt Damon was the only one in *Saving Private Ryan* who didn't go through 10-days of boot camp basic training led by a Marine veteran. This was done so the other actors would show resentment towards him, to fit the onscreen character dynamics.

985. The line-up in *The Usual Suspects* was originally meant to be serious, but Benicio del Toro couldn't stop farting so they laughed throughout.

986. Michelle Pfeiffer was literally vacuum-sealed into her Catwoman costume for *Batman Returns*, which, as you might imagine, made it very difficult to move and breathe. To top it off, the outfit's razor-sharp claws were incredibly difficult to work with. Pfeiffer consistently found herself caught on various parts of the set.

987. It took two-and-a-half hours a day to apply Lon Chaney's makeup in *The Hunchback of Notre Dame*.

988. The movie *Titanic* cost more money to film than the actual ship cost to build. It worked out in the end, as the film earned $1.8 billion worldwide and scored 11 Oscars.

989. Chris Farley was originally cast as Shrek, and he even recorded part of the movie, but he was replaced by Mike Myers after he died of a drug overdose.

990. The Motion Picture Association of America would not allow use of the name 'Focker' for the film *Meet the Fockers* unless the filmmakers could find an actual person with that last name.

991. In 2002, Steven Spielberg finally finished college after a 33-year hiatus. He turned in *Schindler's List* for his student film requirement.

992. The Michael Myers face mask in *Halloween* is Captain Kirk/William Shatner death mask, created for *Star Trek*, that's painted white.

993. Gal Gadot was actually five months pregnant while filming the reshoots for *Wonder Woman*. The costume department had to cut a section out of the front of her costume and replace it with green cloth so her figure could be altered in postproduction.

994. The dog who played Toto in *The Wizard of Oz* received a higher salary than most of those who played Munchkins. She received $125 a week, while the Munchkins received between $50-$100.

995. The pile of feces that Jamal jumps into in *Slumdog Millionaire* is a mix of chocolate and peanut butter.

996. In the film, Scarface, an M16 assault rifle with an M203 40mm grenade launcher attached to the barrel is Tony's "little friend."

997. In the 1979 version of "Mad Max", they ran low on funds. Director George Miller offered his own vehicle for one of the crash scenes.

998. In Home Alone, when Kevin finds a picture of Buzz's girlfriend, is actually a picture of a boy dressed as a girl. Director Chris Columbus thought it would be too cruel to make fun of a girl in that way. The boy that was used in the photo was the art director's son.

999. Justin Hurwitz, the musical composer of *La La Land*, wrote over 1,900 piano demos for director Damien Chazelle to discover the correct melodies for the film.

1000. The post-production sound team of *Hacksaw Ridge* used a variety of sounds to mimic gun fire, including bumble bees, a Lamborghini, and dry ice melting.

Conclusion

Thank you for taking the time to read this book. I hope that you enjoyed these fun facts and learn some new things in the process! There are an infinite number of other facts and bits of information out there that we have yet to learn about. This should inspire all of us to take the time to try and learn something new every day.

Made in the USA
Coppell, TX
11 September 2023

21475033R00073